Frank E. Ormsby

The Law and the Prophets

A scientific work

Frank E. Ormsby

The Law and the Prophets
A scientific work

ISBN/EAN: 9783337240851

Printed in Europe, USA, Canada, Australia, Japan

Cover: Foto ©Lupo / pixelio.de

More available books at **www.hansebooks.com**

"THE LAW AND THE PROPHETS"

A SCIENTIFIC WORK

ON THE RELATIONSHIP BETWEEN PHYSICAL BODIES, VEGETABLE, ANIMAL, HUMAN, AND PLANETARY.

DESIGNED FOR THE INSTRUCTION AND GUIDANCE OF STUDENTS IN THE

OCCULT SCIENCES

BY

FRANK EARL ORMSBY,

A MAGIAN MYSTIC.

ILLUSTRATED.

1893,
CHICAGO.

CONTENTS.

Preface,	7
Introduction,	11
Diagram No. 1,	14
The Zodiac,	15
The Significance of the Signs,	16 to 29
Polarities and Aspects,	29
The Zodiac and Planets,	30
Waves of Energy,	31
Comparative Vibrations,	33
Significance of the Planets,	34 to 44
An Error,	44
Diagram No. 3,	45
Concerning Delineation,	46
Solar Anatomy,	47
Diagram No. 4,	48
Symbolism,	49
Aspects of the Planets,	54
Diagram No. 5,	56
Condensed Statements,	57
Diagram No. 6,	59
Delineations,	60 to 96
Diagnosing Diseases,	97 to 121
Abraham Lincoln,	123
George Francis Train,	124
Robert G. Ingersoll,	126

CONTENTS.

Questions and Answers,	131
" " " continued,	140
Lesson in Questions,	148
Physical Life,	150
Cause of Diseases,	151
How to Eat,	152
Prayer Illustrated,	157
Dinner Fit for the Gods,	159
A Word to the Seeker,	163
Individual Astral Vibration,	165
Phrenology and Physiognomy,	178
Magnetic Co-Ordination Chart,	184
An Ideal Character,	188
Incarnations,	191
The Adept,	192
Spiritually,	194
Concering Tables,	195
Concerning Mechanical Chart,	196
The Black Star,	199
Correction Tables,	200
Percentage Tables,	204
Astronomical Figures,	205
Conclusion,	210

PREFACE.

There should be but one object in life, and that one object should be to elevate, not only, the human race, but every race and species of animal, vegetable, and mineral life, and bring the same into a higher and better condition. It is impossible to raise the human races, and allow the lower forms to remain. It is also impossible to raise the lower creations, and bring them into more nearly perfect expression, without sooner or later, having the fact clearly illustrated, that what is possible in physical developement with the animal races, may be a hundred times more so upon the human plane of expression.

The breeding of horses, cattle, chickens and swine, as well as the cultivation of fruits and vegetables, has been reduced to a practical science, and it is with supreme pleasure and profit, that we view and contemplate the manifestations in these directions, all of which is the result of experiment, experience, and knowledge of the law which governs generic qualities in these varied lines. The law of animal life has been studied by some so closely, and carefully, that they can read the life of a horse at a glance, and give every physical, as well as mental characteristic of the animal.

There is but one thing lacking to make the science of character delineation with the animal kingdom perfect, and that is an understand-

PREFACE.

ing of the vibratory, or magnetic forces, which operate upon, aye,—control all physical organisms—human, animal, vegetable and mineral. Some argue that it hurts the soul life of things, to change them from their natural course, and that the mining of gold even, and the processes of refining, casting, hammering and polishing, (which certainly raises it into a higher condition and expression,) is in reality bad for the real life of the gold; but the soul of man is also hurt, apparently, by the processes of education, cultivation, growth and refinement, together with the trials in business tribulations; yet who can say that he has not been benefitted by the process!

The lower forms of physical life have had sufficient attention for a time, therefore this work is dedicated to the human race, and is more particularly intended for those who are and wish to become qualified to minister unto the masses, as Teachers, Physicians, Healers, and Clergymen, as well as those who delve deeply into Mystic Secrets, and seek to know the meaning of things unseen by many, with the physical eye, and only known through a knowledge of what has been termed, "The Secret Doctrine," "The Hidden Light," "Wisdom of the East," "Revelation," "Illumination," "The Central Flame," and many other occult phrases, all of which are expressions concerning *One Law*, viz.— The law of physical environments. Observe the plural. The author believes that such information as is practical and valuable to struggling humanity in every day life, concerning the *Law*, should be arranged and expressed in plain simple terms, that all may understand its true meaning and significance.

Many who have sought and found the secret key that unlocks the door of the treasure-house, which holds the secret wisdom, have in attempting to make personal application of the lessons gained, become extremists; have isolated themselves from all conditions existing in the customs and practices of the times; in fact have ceased to be of any service to themselves or to the world in which they live. They sought

PREFACE.

for power. To do something for the world is the object and aim of the author of this work.

Astrology, so called, which has been practiced by many unscrupulous pretenders for many years, is generally understood to mean fortune-telling. The abuse of the science of the stars, by those who have thus attempted to foretell future events, and answer personal questions, giving exact dates, and hours, for the fulfillment of certain business, as well as other promises, the number of husbands, wives, and even children that a person will have, as well as other equally foolish pretended information, leads me to state: *No man knoweth the future*, except in a general way. The personal acts of an individual cannot be determined by the stars. The *personal feelings* of every individual may be, but their acts under the impulses given by such feelings, *no man can foretell*. It can be foretold what is *Best* for a person to do, under the law at any future date. But just what will be done must be determined by the surrounding environment at the time. This no man can determine.

For reasons given, I drop the term Astrology, and use the title given to this work. "The Law and the Prophets." "The Law" signifies the eternal fixed principles in nature. "The Prophets" signify the students of the Law, who become Prophets as they attain to an understanding of the Law. Through our physical organisms we must learn the meaning of the Law, and with the application of this science to the physical structure, man,—comes the Prophetic gifts. Those who are wise, and well versed in this science, have a higher and holier mission in the world, than that of telling fortunes or catering to the ignorant, who implore the Gods to lead them to material wealth and pleasure.

This work pertains to the science of Phrenology, Physiognomy, Physiology, and all of the forces related to the Physique of man. From the standpoint of Physiogony.—"Birth by Nature." This work is intended as a formal introduction of *souls* to the Universe. Simplicity is the word which we should ever have in mind, when devoting our time

PREFACE.

to the study of life and its problems. The more we study, and the more we learn, the more we see, how simple is the *Law;* therefore, the attention of the student is called by the drawings and explanations contained in this work, to the wonderful power to be gained, through an understanding of very simple forces.

That the studies and experiences of those who enter into this line of investigation may be fraught with pleasure, profit, and wisdom, and that a new era will some day be brought about through a more general understanding of these wonderful laws of life, is the wish, the intense desire, and belief of the

AUTHOR.

OUR EARLY EXPERIENCES.

INTRODUCTION.

What is law? Sir Isaac Newton re-discovered the great infinite truth concerning the law of matter, (as we understand matter, or substance,) which is, that every particle of matter in the universe attracts every other particle, according to its density, and inversely according to the square of its distance, which is acknowledged by all scientists, as demonstrable.

This being true, there must be a power, force, or energy, inherent in the particle of matter, which gives it the attractive quality, and magnetic vibration, is the term I will use to express the idea of this force or energy, to those who are ready to admit that there is an inherent life or power co-existent with the atom.

What is vibration? It is infinite and eternal activity, motion, expression, and repetition. It is manifest not only in matter as we view material things, or substance, but the boundless spaces are alive and teeming with this eternal principle.

The ether of space which is in a state of vibration so high that no mechanical instrument, or chemical composition can be produced to record the number of waves per second (because matter or gasses vibrated that high would become ether, and cease to exist as matter or even gas,) and which permeates all substances, and in which all substances act, in transmitting their effects to and upon all other substances, is the wire, or vacuum, through which the messages,—that is to say, magnetic influences, forces or powers, pass from atom to atom, planet to planet, and sun to sun.

INTRODUCTION.

The fact that light, which is a very high vibration, considered from a physical standpoint, requires time to pass from one point to another, and from one planet to another, proves conclusively that the ether of space is in a state of activity, and through its apparent static condition, compared with material substances, light can travel but 186,000 miles per second, whereas, if space is a vacuum in the absolute, there would be no limit to the speed of light.

The ultimate atom, or smallest particle of matter discoverable by man, has been found to be globular, and reasoning from the known and provable, to the unknown and unprovable, except through the development of the intuitive faculties which gives one the power of soul recognition in matters of a universal nature, it can reasonably be stated that the matter contained in the atom is surrounding a force from the fact, that a little higher in the scale of globular expression, a point is pressed out, and is known to take hold of other substance, absorb the same, digest and pass it away; showing conclusively that an intelligent force dwells within the atom.

The law of material bodies, re-stated by Newton, draws atoms together, and in doing so there comes a time when these atoms get into close quarters, and friction produces physical heat and fire, finally resulting in the formation of worlds, suns and systems, to be blotted out and reproduced in other forms and combinations as the cycles roll on.

As each atom of matter affects every other atom, so each human being affects every other human being, and each planet and sun, which are aggregations of atoms, affect every other planet and sun. Each human being is a magnet with attractive and repellant powers or qualities. Every planet and sun is also a magnet, having both attractive and repellant qualities.

It has taken many ages of observation and experiment, to find out how much, and what kind of effects are produced by the action of other planets in our system, in their different relations to the earth, and the

INTRODUCTION.

human organism, which is made from the dust,—the atoms, of the earth, has been the instrument through which these forces and influences, have been tested, and brought within the understanding of man. After ages of research and study in occult lines of investigation, a system has been perfected, by which the powers of the different planets in our system can be determined. This is the result of mathematics, hence is provable.

The Zodiac is the scale, or measure, which is the foundation for the working out of different, and varying effects, resulting from the changes in distance and polarity constantly being produced. Human organisms are made up of the atoms of the earth, therefore we are earth magnets, partaking of the magnetic condition of the earth. Whatever changes are produced in the magnetic condition of the earth, produces a like change in the condition of all human magnets upon it.

The Zodiac, which represents the polarity of the earth, and its relation to the sun, is the scale therefore, by which are measured the forces in nature so far as they relate to, or effect human life upon this planet. This introductory declaration of principles according to the highest authorities in all branches of scientific research, was deemed necessary, that a beginning in this line of study might have the backing or support of the acknowledged scientific minds of both the past and present.

The lessons contained herein, which follow these declarations of universal principles, will relate to what is called Occult Astronomy, Occult Forces, Hidden Wisdom, etc., and must not be confounded with material astronomy, as explained by the material astronomers of OUR TIME.

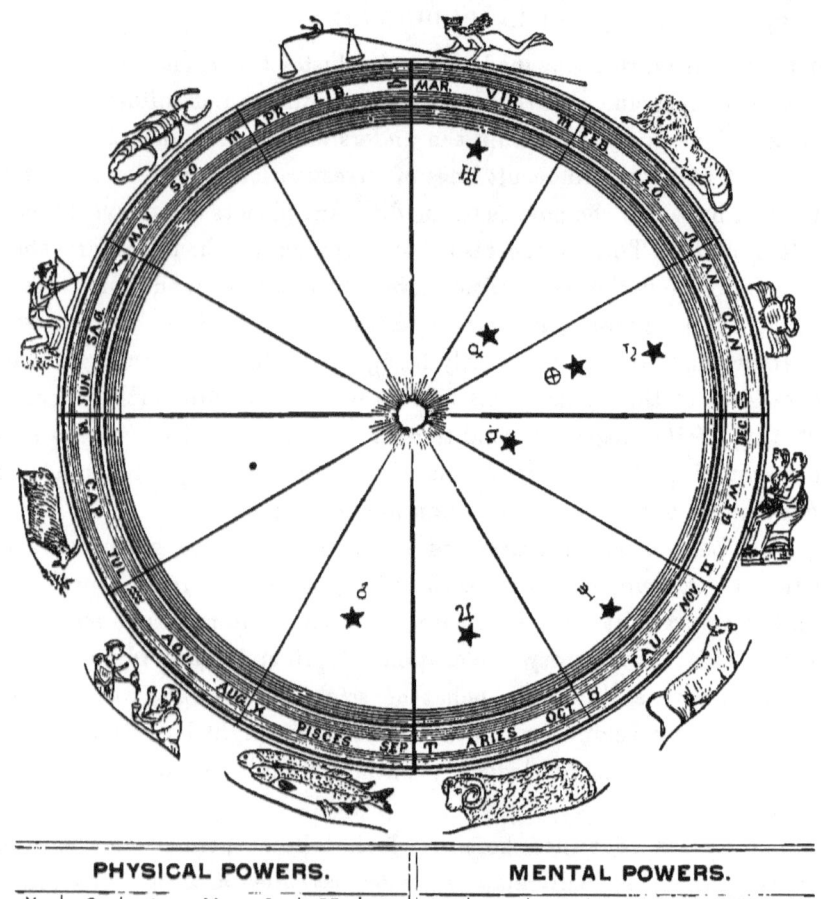

DIAGRAM No. 1.

"THE LAW AND THE PROPHETS."

LESSON ONE.

The Zodiac represents the divisions, sections, or parts of our solar system, the meridians of which show where these sections meet, just the same as the sections of an orange, enclose a certain amount of liquid and seeds, each laying close to another section, yet distinctly separate. Some of these sections vary somewhat from thirty degrees. Why this is so in the divisions of our solar system, is accounted for by the theory, that the converging rays of each constellation of stars vibrating to our Sun, forms a conic section, the outlines of which have been traced, and their true meridian found, and this theory also accounts for the different effects of each house, or division, on the ground that as some constellations are nearer than others, some with more stars and of different densities, their combinations produce an entirely different vibration in each division. This same theory also accounts for the fact that the effect of a planet is the same in any part of a sign or section, and as all of these things are accounted for by this theory, it is safe to declare as a fact, that the constellations, whose conis divided by a line, the meridian that separates Aries from Taurus, and this illustration represents an actual division in the anatomy of man. The very hour that a certain planet crosses that line that rules strong at the time of the birth of a very sensitive person, can be determined by the peculiar change of vibration at this division of the head. Aries is the first sign in what is called the quarter of love or affection in the four divisions of the heavens.

TAURUS.

While Aries has been found to rule mental qualities and functions of the brain, Taurus, in like manner, has been found to have the quality of vitality, energy, physical and muscular strength, and nerve force. That portion of mans anatomy represented as belonging to that division (see diagram,) is that part of the physical organism where the nervous system centers at the base of the back or lower brain. The muscular system also centers there. Hence, all that portion of the system, included in that sign, covering the throat, tonsils, lower brain, or cerebellum. The nerve centers and muscular powers, are controlled by the sign Taurus. The sign Taurus therefore represents physical force and energy.

SPECIAL SIGNIFICANCE OF TAURUS.

Persons born in Taurus, usually have a great amount of physical force, energy, enterprise, and ability to carry on business and make successes on the physical plane. The aspect of other planets to this house must always be considered before any judgement as to character can be safely given. Some planets aspecting this house, cause persons to be lazy and opposed to work of every kind.

Taurus is a very important sign to take into consideration, in physical delineations, because it represents the nervous and muscular sytems. All diseases of the nervous system including tonsilitis, sore throat, catarrh, diphtheria, coughs and colds, nervous prostration, and the first stages of consumption, are found and treated by this system through calculations made of the aspects, powers and positions of the planets and Earth as related to this sign. It is at this point in the human organism that all colds contracted are allowed to enter the system.

GEMINI.

Gemini represents that section in the construction of mans physical body, in which the upper part of the lungs are connected to the windpipe.

[NOTE.—This is stated in this manner to explain why Gemini governs the lungs, when the lungs are principally in the house of Cancer and even extend into the sign Leo, and surround the heart. It must be remembered that lung difficulties originate in the windpipe and shut off the circulation leading to the lungs proper, therefore Gemini covers the section which includes the windpipe and connection with the lungs.]

The lungs are strong or weak according to the aspects of the planets to the sign Gemini, the same as mentioned concerning other houses.

SPECIAL FEATURES OF GEMINI.

Gemini is called the house of marriage from the fact that persons born in this sign, are home bodies generally, and prefer married to single life.

They are usually quiet people, and not very expressive, rather reserved. They are adapted to the home, and make excellent fathers and mothers. They are domestic, honorable and upright.

Country life, or the life of a small village will suit them much better than the city. The diseases of the different houses are treated in the readings given farther on. Gemini completes the quarter of love and affection, hence it is doubly appropriate to call it the house of unions or marriage.

CANCER.

Is that division or section of the system which includes the chest. The mammaries, the mammary arteries and veins, which in the female are very much more vital than in the male.

Physical disturbances which result from a bad aspect to this house, are always centered in the chest, and cancer, the cause of which will be fully explained later on, is the main symptoms or result. Cancer is the first sign in the quarter of wisdom. Cancer being in quadratic aspect to the sign Aries, has not only its own force and condition, but this strong aspect gives it an added impulse and influence from the sign Aries, therefore this house is second in expression, invention, activity, positiveness, perception, intuition, etc.

SPECIAL FEATURES OF CANCER.

Persons born in Cancer are quick, bright, intellectual, and they take great interest in educational matters. They are also progressive and liberal in their views, are natural business characters, and make careful financiers. They also make good professional men, and when the sign is well aspected, good orators, preachers, lawyers, and teachers. They have scientific tendencies, and are inventive, and original in thought and expression. The Earth is in perihelion in this house, therefore the physical constitutions of those born in this sign are very enduring. Cancer is not a vital section in the anatomy of man, therefore the significance of the sign Cancer applies more to the intellect.

LEO.

Leo is next in order, and this section encloses the heart, —that is the vital portion of the heart,—as the heart and lungs are closely related. The reason that Leo is the sign of the heart is because the apex of the heart points downward. The apex is that point or portion of the heart where the positive and negative poles of the atoms of the blood meet, unite, blend, and harmonize, and spring forth again to vitalize and vivify the system.

What Aries means to the mental man, Leo means to the physical man. For Leo is the most vital of all the signs or sections in the human organism. Life on the physical plane depends entirely upon the action of the heart. Heart failure is the principle difficulty in this section or sign. Symptoms appear in different parts of the system as the result of the aspect of some planets to the sign Leo, which derange the blood and circulation, and cause inharmony throughout the system.

The health therefore depends upon the quantity, quality, and circulation of this life fluid, and because of this the sign Leo has been named the sign of power, intelligence, and strength.

SPECIAL FEATURES OF LEO.

All who are born when the Earth is in Leo, have marked characteristics, and strong mental powers, they love intellectual pursuits, and are the compilers, historians and writers of the age in which they live. They express more with the pen, and less with the vocal organs, generally, while Cancer people are vocalists.

Leo represents one of the points of the Pyramid, which expresses the living fire of life, the sacred flame of the intelligence of the soul, from which proceedeth the ray that leadeth ever on, and on. * * * *

The Zodiac has three crosses or quadrates. Aries, Cancer, Libra, and Capricorus, form the positive Cross. Taurus, Leo, Scorpio and Acquarius form the Vital Cross.

Gemini, Virgo, Sagittarius and Pisces form the Negative Cross, or quadrate.

The Positive Cross represents the male.
The Vital Cross represents the Female.
The Negative Cross represents Neutrality.

VIRGO.

Virgo is the last house in the quarter of Wisdom, and means to the physical body that section which includes the stomach, kidneys and liver, which is a very vital section in the composition of our bodies.

Through this section comes nearly all of the suffering that flesh is heir to. The stomach receives from without all that is taken to keep the inner flame burning. Therefore, the vibrations of the inner man are according to the effect of the substances thus taken.

If the sign Virgo is afflicted by a combination of planets in strong aspect, whose vibrations are not harmoniously blended, there is a weakness in that section, and indigestion results, causing kidney and liver difficulties first, and a general constipated condition throughout the system later.

SPECIAL FEATURES OF VIRGO.

Persons born in Virgo are very emotional in their natures. They have vivid imaginations, spiritual tendencies, ideal thoughts and desires. The virgin is the symbol of this house, and virtue is one of the main characteristics of those born here. The desire for the higher and more spiritual conditions, leads Virgo people into studies that the ordinary student will not readily grasp. Virgo is the most spirtualizing in effect upon human thoughts and desires of any of the signs, hence, they have religious tendencies very marked, and prophetic vision clear and distinct.

LIBRA.

Libra represents the section that includes the bowels, the first degree of which starts at the navel, the place of the umbilical cord, which is the solar center of the physical body, and is called the Solar Plexus.

This sign represents the material in life and expression. The entire physical structure is built up through this center, or connection with the universal forces. As Libra expresses physical conditions principally, all things of a material and worldly nature are polarized to this section, and business of every kind is included in the significance of this sign. The Earth bears the same relation as to polarity in this house that she does in Aries, and this is her third position for mental activity, especially in latitudes north of the equator.

SPECIAL FEATURES OF LIBRA.

Persons born while the Earth is in Libra, are the best balanced physically and are more harmonious and cheerful than those born in any other sign. There seems to be a more perfect poise in their physical make up. They seem to stand, as it were, between the spiritual and the material, as if they were just balanced by these conditions in life. Hence the sign of the Scales, the Balances, is placed here to symbolize that dominant characteristic.

Libra is the first house in the quarter of wealth, and those born here desire wealth and seek in every physical way to obtain it. Traders and merchants generally are born best in this house.

SCORPIO.

Scorpio signifies the section which includes the Generative Organs, the bladder, womb, colon, and orifices of this region, and is the opposite, or negative pole of the nervous and muscular center of the system, being opposite Taurus. This sign is also in quadratic aspect, to the sign Leo, which rules the circulation of the blood, all of which make Scorpio a very vital sign, or section in the human structure. It means much to persons born in this sign, whether there are bad combinations of forces acting upon it or not, because when this sign is afflicted, Leo, and Taurus are also affected, hence the conditions at birth may be very good or very bad, while the Earth is passing through this section.

SPECIAL FEATURES OF SCORPIO.

All who are born in this sign, are sowers; they are workers, and are always planning for future returns,—"Casting their bread upon the waters," as it were. When the Earth is in Scorpio, it is the season of planting and sowing, and persons born here naturally partake of the general atmosphere of the time and its labors.

This sign signifies physical expression generally, and those who are born in Scorpio are not mental giants, and never orators, unless Aries has the support of two or more planets capable of producing the power and quality necessary to make an orator, and even then, the result will not be as great as when the Earth is also in aspect to Aries. Persons born in this house make good workers, fair financiers, especially in private matters and investments.

SAGITTARIUS.

We have passed below the vital regions in the anatomy of man, when we reach Sagittarius, so far as the signs are concerned, but the aspect or relation to the vital signs makes Sagittarius, in a way, quite important in calculating the characteristics of persons born while the Earth is passing through it.

Sagittarius includes a section of our bodies that reaches from the hip joints down just below the muscles of the legs about four inches above the knee joint, and signifies strength, endurance, firmness, independence, morality, and regularity, and on account of these qualities persons who are born here, are quite apt to lead single lives. They are somewhat opposed to married life. The position of the sign is in opposition to the house of marriage and unions.

SPECIAL FEATURES OF SAGITTARIUS.

The general tendency of all who are born in this sign is to celibacy, and as single life makes one more free to travel and see the world, Sagittarius characters are inclined to travel. They are quiet and reserved, talk but little, and measure well their words and sentences.

Rheumatic difficulties are the physical disturbances which occur in this section.

This is the last house in the quarter of wealth and business, therefore these characters are not as good for business as those born in the two previous signs.

CAPRICORNUS.

Capricornus includes the knees, and as this is the first sign in the quarter of labor, how perfectly it represents the most important and active joint or section, used in physical exercise.

As this sign signifies labor, is in opposition aspect to Cancer, the intellectual sign, and in quadrature to Libra, the physical sign, also to Aries, the sign of expression, it is one of the most important sections in the divisions of our systems, especially in affairs relating to physical needs and requirements, and mental qualities for obtaining the same. Business men, and leaders in large undertakings, which require an immense amount of labor and capitol are born here.

SPECIAL FEATURES OF CAPRICORNUS.

Persons born in this sign are active workers, powerful characters, with large, broad views, intelligent, very attentive to their own business, always busy, and always making money, except when a bad combination of planetary forces is upon them. They are leaders in large undertakings, and make excellent bosses in enterprises, requiring skill in that direction. Large contract work suits them best, as a business, although many born here enter the mercantile lines, as traders.

AQUARIUS.

Acquarius includes the calves of the limbs, is the center section in the quarter of labor, and is quite a vital sign on account of the aspect to Leo, Taurus and Scorpio.

When Acquarius is well aspected by the planets, the best workers are born, and they are so intense in their ambition and desire to work, that they are never idle a moment. Plans are laid ahead for days, as to what will be done next.

Paralysis is the main physical derangement which crops out in persons born in this sign, but only when the sign is afflicted, which will be explained in the future readings of this work.

SPECIAL FEATURES OF AQUARIUS.

Persons born here, as said before, are the best workers, and they are bound to work whether it pays or not. They have an immense amount of surplus energy, and on account of this, they are usually hard people to get along with unless properly mated.

Take ten persons born in Aquarius, and ten born in Aries, with equal aspects from the planets, and put them to work on a job, and the Aquarius crew would do all the work and be willing to, for the pleasure of hearing the Aries crew tell stories and give their ideas concerning the advisability of getting up some mechanical contrivance to do the work for them, so they could sit and watch it.

PISCES.

Pisces is the last sign, and section in these great divisions in nature, and especially in the physical structures of human beings. It includes the ankles and feet, the last five degrees more particularly effect the toes. Corns and bunions are the result of an affliction to this sign, and to these five degrees.

Pisces is considered the house of the understanding, as it represents the negative pole of our solar system and the negative pole of the human organism.

Being negative indicates low vitality, and weakness, compared with Cancer or Leo.

SPECIAL FEATURES OF PISCES.

All who are born in Pisces are destined to be on their feet the biggest part of the time through life, their feet seem to be the most active part of them. They are always standing or walking. Never quite satisfied when sitting.

They are usually negative, receptive, and mediumistic. They seek the ideal, but are firm upon the physical foundation. They are usually good workers, and are very artistic. Their judgment is very good. They say but little, in fact they are the most quiet in this respect of any of the twelve manner of people.

SIGNS.

These signs or sections of the human organism are the same, magnetically that the same signs or sections in the divisions of the solar circle are. The human sections are the result of the other, hence, God made man in his own image, and the heavenly man, the divine man, the all powerful being is eternal in the heavens, and abideth forever. It is the combinations of forces operating from the planets of our solar system to the Sun, and reflected to the Earth, that cause our weak and strong points, and special traits of character. The divisions of our bodies are always the same, and are the direct counterpart of the heavens, that is the solar system, after the first breath of life, air, magnetic force, vibration, or energy of the universe is taken into the lungs.

If the currents of magnetic power from Saturn and Mercury, or Saturn and Neptune are operating strong upon any sign in the heavens, and no other planets which serve to counteract these forces, are in aspect to the same house, or to the Earth, at the time a child is born, that section of the solar system is in a bad vibratory state, or condition, and as the child is magnetically stamped at the time of birth, the section of the organism corresponding to the solar section will be charged with the magnetic force and quality of that section, and no other, therefore the physical organisms of human beings have been the Hygrometers, or Psychometrical instruments, which have tested, and determined to the fraction of a degree the influences, powers, forces, qualities, and relations of the magnets of our solar system. Wonderful indeed, is this achievement, and well may we turn with respect, and admiration to the genius of prehistoric times, when souls that are now in the flesh as well as those who dwell in spiritual states, were the embodied builders and carvers of these great, grand, and universal statements and symbols concerning the nature of God and man.

POLARITIES AND ASPECTS.

As the polarity of the Earth, which is the Earth's position in each sign and the angle at which she receives vibrations from the Sun, determines the development, powers, and characteristics of people, to a certain extent, so does each of the other planets in our solar system, also determine qualities, and traits of character, when they are in the different signs.

The aspects of all the planets to the Earth, and vital signs, determine the physical conditions in human life, while the aspects to the sign Aries, determine the mental powers, qualities, and degrees of expression. The delineation of the sign Aries is the science of planetary phrenology, while the delineation of all the signs, is the science of planetary physiology, or anatomy. The science of planetary physiognomy which is a deeper knowledge of magnetic effects is also confined to the sign Aries and aspects thereto.

So the nature of planetary forces, polarities, and aspects, are dual, and must be considered from two distinct standpoints, namely, physical and mental.

Aries, Taurus, Gemini, Cancer, Leo and Virgo, cover the vital sections in the human organism, and they are in the right half of the Zodiac, the other six signs are below the solar plexus or center, and are called the physical or negative divisions, comparatively, and they cover the left half of the Zodiac.

Aries is the mental sign positive. The exact opposite in principle, as well as position is the greatest physical sign Libra, which is the physical sign positive.

Taurus is the most powerful in nerve force and muscular strength, Scorpio is the weakest, just the opposite.

Gemini represents unions, marriage, and home life and principles, while Sagittarius signifies single life, traveling, etc.

Cancer signifies knowledge, science, art, etc., while Capricornus means material expression, coarse, and bulky traffic and enterprise. Leo represents wisdom, and genius, while Aquarius, means physical expression, and labor.

Virgo represents the spiritual, the ideal in human life, while Pisces leads to the Earthly state. These relations represent the positive and negative principle manifested throughout the universe, which is the *Divine* Logos of the Infinite Life.

THE ZODIAC AND PLANETS.

Diagram No. 1 shows the scale or measure by which the powers and aspects of the planets are determined.

The planets are shown in their perihelion houses, that is, their nearest position to the Sun, which is their closest magnetic relation to that center. They are the farthest, therefore the weakest, when they reach the house, or sign opposite. Hence, the Earth is farthest from the Sun, and weakest magnetically or physically, when in Capricornus. Likewise Saturn, whose perihelion home is the same sign as that of the Earth, which is Cancer.

The planets all move from Aries to the right around the Sun.

WAVES OF ENERGY.

The effects of the planets upon the Earth are the result of the throbbings of their bodies, producing vibrations which traverse the ether of space and strike the Sun repeating their force, the same as the clicks of numerous telegraph instruments are repeated at the central office.

These are waves of energy, force, activity, power, and vitality, and as the Earth is connected by wire to the central Orb, the messages sent in from the stars are repeated to the Earth.

These waves are illustrated in Plate No. 2, which gives, in a crude way, the comparative powers of the different waves as received by the Earth.

Mercury vibrates very high, on account of its density and rapidity of motion through space, also nearness to the Sun. Remember the Earth senses the condition of the Sun as produced by the magnets acting thereon.

Take hold of an electric battery with a very strong current turned on, and the effect will be to cause you to make a change at once, you will not stop to think it over, or consider the matter for a moment. The vibrations of Mercury have about the same influence on the minds of men. They are quick, active, changeable, flighty and hilarious. Every vibration from Mercury strikes with a point as shown by the star.

Venus vibrations are in comparison, like the affect of a battery when it is just right to be pleasant to the senses, soothing, as it were. Hence Venus has a harmonizing influence upon the Earth's magnetism, and upon the physical organisms, and mental and vocal expressions of human beings. The waves of Venus are represented as being finer, longer and more elastic. Venus strikes smoothly at all times, as represented by the circle.

Mars' waves are like Mercury's in force, but like Venus' in quantity, hence represents a combination, or quality between the two.

Mars beats just hard enough to make people combative, and causes them to feel like striking back. Mars strikes with points which mean trouble some times, and at others with the flat, even surface as shown by the pyramid.

Jupiter has longer, more powerful, yet somewhat elastic waves, like Venus in kind, but slower and more powerful in action and effect.

Jupiter strikes with a cushioned mallet, but there are curves and edges to these cushions into which people are drawn and absorbed. It is the nature of Jupiter people to absorb in a smooth easy manner the accumulations and earnings of others, hence the cushioned circle is used to symbolize his beats upon the Sun, Earth, and human beings.

Saturn has the heaviest and most vital sting of all, and is the disintegrater of every thing that will yield to his beats, which are represented by many points, which pick to pieces the flesh of man.

Uranus has a very deliberate, fine, and intense wave, like unto Venus in fineness, but more like Mars in intensity. It strikes squarely and softly generally, but Uranus has points which will turn and combat with inharmonious forces, and when the points of Mars are operating in conjunction with Uranus, the points of Uranus respond, and trouble appears in the lives of those who are related to such an aspect.

Neptune has fine vibrations, but they are long drawn out

in effect. Their influence is to cause people to reach out, travel across the ocean, visit foreign lands, penetrate, as illustrated, into other spheres.

These illustrations are given merely to impress the student with the comparative force and influence of each planet. They are not used in delineations, but are intended for the training of the mind.

COMPARATIVE VIBRATIONS.

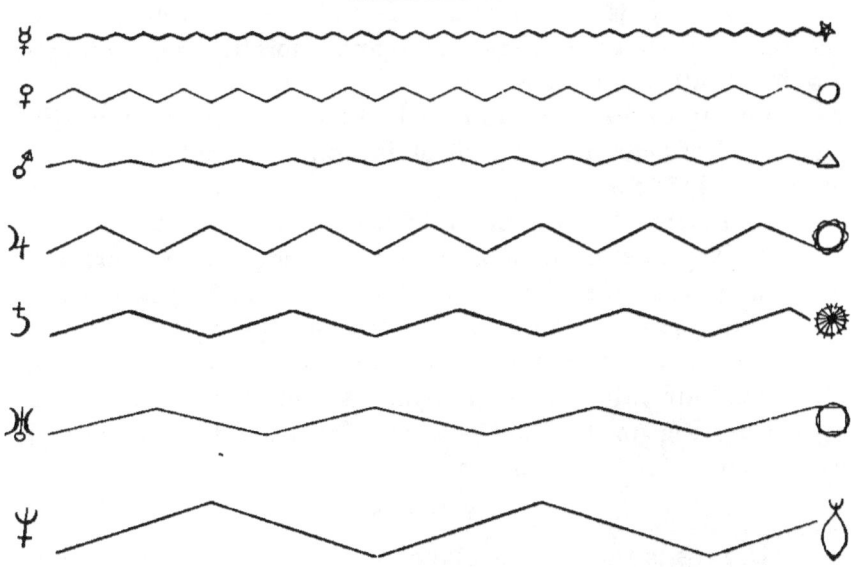

SIGNIFICANCE OF THE PLANETS.

NEPTUNE.

Neptune was the first planet formed in our solar system, and being the outermost planet, the vibrations from that source operate more forcibly upon the outer covering of the body, the skin and hair, exemplifying the great law of affinity, expressed throughout nature.

Neptune is the protector, the sentinal from without, the developer of the larger thoughts and functions of the brain, and like the large body and immense distance from the Sun, so are the impulses, desires and feelings of Neptune people. Self-esteem, conscience, firmness and morality, are phrenological traits of character.

Owing to the desire to travel which Neptune produces in the mind of man, all business of international interest comes under its influence.

Commerce, and travel, at home and abroad, cause us to look to Neptune in financial matters of that nature, therefore, Neptune is considered a financial planet. As Neptune rules the skin, and as colds are contracted through the same, which result sometimes in pneumonia, pleurisy, inflammations, bronchial difficulties, rheumatism, gout, etc. Neptune has a great bearing upon all of these complaints, and when Saturn is in aspect, it means serious trouble.

URANUS.

Uranus is the second planet formed in our system, and the impulse given us by that magnet, creates the desire to be actively engaged in some labor, requiring scientific experiments and research. Most of the scientists in all ages of the world have been strongly influenced by the planet Uranus. Students of the Occult, who make any great success in gaining real knowledge in that branch of learning, are strongly influenced, and magnetically charged at the time of birth.

The vibrations of this planet do not give one the desire for wealth, power, and glory, but rather influences the mind or soul, to consider the deeper and inner meanings of life, and the possibilities of growth and attainment spiritually. Uranus therefore is called the spiritual and religious planet, as well as the planet of labor.

The nervous system of man is directly under the influence of this magnet, and as the center or positive pole of the nerves is connected or located at the base of the brain, Uranus is the planet effecting the brain, and is called the ruler of the brain.

In some positions and aspects, Uranus produces clairvoyant sight, intuition, and the condition necessary to inspiration. Seers and Prophets of old as well as those of our time are favorably blessed with the influence of Uranus.

The phrenological points are veneration, benevolence, sublimity, spirituality, honesty and integrity.

All nervous diseases are largely the result of Uranus when afflicted by Saturn, Mars, or Neptune, with Mercury in the combination.

SATURN.

Saturn was the third planet formed, and owing to the cross currents of his moons, and rings, eleven in number, the magnetic or vibrant force from such a combination is very disturbing in its nature, and the effect is inharmony, dissatisfaction, sickness and sorrow, in human lives, that are strongly related to Saturn at birth. Saturn causes people to be repulsive, at the same time very tenacious and persistant in everything they attempt to do.

On account of the disturbing quality of Saturn's power, more real education, growth, and advancement comes from that source, than from any other planet in our system. His effect upon the physical and vital organs of human beings is very bad, however, and nearly all the ills that flesh is heir to, are traceable to his vibrations. For this reason Saturn is called the ruler of the flesh and bones. The most noticeable effect of Saturn's influence upon the system, is stricture, which seems to draw together the arteries and veins, as well as the ducts, and cause a clogging, and stoppage of the circulation, producing a feverish condition in the parts afflicted, and forming a sort of a pool, or catch basin, into which the grosser, and impure portions of the blood lodge, the final result being brain fever, consumption, cancer, heart disease, liver complaint, secret disorders, rheumatism, corns and bunions, and various other diseases too numerous to mention.

Selfishness, secretiveness, caution, inharmony, continuity, tenacity, and determination are phrenological characteristics.

Saturn is the principle planet to consider in physical delineation.

JUPITER.

Jupiter was the fourth magnet formed in our system, and being by far the largest of any, is called the ruler of the solar system. Like the large and powerful planet that he is, so are the people who are strongly influenced by the vibrant power of his pulsations. They have large ideas of physical things and business generally, and are constantly seeking to rule the commercial interests of the world. They seek riches, and devote their powers, which are great, if Jupiter is well placed with the other planets and the Earth, to the gaining of wealth.

For this reason money seems to come to Jupiter characters very easy, compared with persons struggling under the influence of Saturn or Uranus.

Jupiter is harmonious in effect upon both the mental and physical man, thus producing harmony and health.

Jupiter being the most powerful material combination in our solar system, he co-ordinates with and controls the same attribute in the organism of man, namely, the muscular fibres of the entire frame. This influence and muscular attraction from Jupiter makes people strong mentally and physically, hence gives greater power to meet the world of business, and win in the battle for gold.

Jupiter people are grasping, but smoothly and harmoniously do they proceed in such undertakings as will give them the opportunity to grasp, and control something.

The phrenological traits and powers are mental force, individuality, acquisitiveness, locality, time, ambition, and physical strength.

Jupiter is called the ruler of money and business.

MARS.

The Planetoids, a ring of small bodies evenly distributed around the sun, do not change sufficiently in their effects to make it possible to figure magnetic forces from them, therefore they are of little importance in delineations.

Mars being the fifth planet formed of sufficient magnitude to figure on, is considered the planet God of War, on account of the peculiar impulse and combative effect of his vibrations.

The warlike attributes of Mars make him a material significator principally, and materiality, physical demonstrations, mathematical proof and accuracy, is demanded to satisfy such natures.

The force and power of Mars makes people warlike, and causes them to become revolutionists whenever extreme conditions are upon a nation. Duels, strikes, quarrels, and bloodshed are the result of Mars' characters yielding to his influence. Mars produces intellectuality, and a commanding mien, and makes people capable and qualified to become leaders in war.

Mars being next to the Earth, outward, co-ordinates with the alimentary canals, and glandular cells of the system. The windpipe, lungs, stomach, intestines, and the orifices are directly affected by a bad aspect.

Mars people do not make wealth, they will not work to obtain it, but are ever seeking position and power, usually combating every proposition that is presented.

Phrenologically, Mars is antagonistic, combative, argumentative, yet possessing conjugality, parental affection, intellectuality, and accuracy.

The Earth, the next planet formed, of which we are a part, furnishes us with nutrition, food and drink.

VENUS.

Venus was the seventh planet formed, hence, is one of the most spiritual and harmonious magnets related to us. She has been named the Goddess of Love, because her vibrant force produces what we call love in human affairs, the affinity of things. Venus does not produce intellectuality to any great extent but the physical effects are intensely pleasing and satisfactory. Venus softens and harmonizes expression, both physical and mental, by producing harmonious conditions throughout the organism.

Venus controls the fluids of the system, especially the spiritual or astral vibrations, from within. She gives persons co-ordinated to her the power and quality, that makes friends, holds customers in business and makes home life harmonious and satisfactory. Venus people are contented, happy, and healthy, generally. On account of the confidence she imparts to those who are born with a high percentage of her power, many suffer from disappointments, caused by misplaced confidence, but they are constituted rightly for suffering, for Venus carries them safely through it, and puts them in condition to suffer again, from other disappointments. Venus people are too honest and trusting, to live in this deceptive world, but the other characters would be ravenous beasts but for the spiritualizing influence of this harmonious and sympathizing magnet.

Venus being yielding in nature, causes people to be the same, therefore appetite and physical desires generally are governed largely by this planet.

Soul force, color, expression, harmony, perception, poetry, tune, faith, hope and charity, are marked traits in the characters of Venus people.

Venus modifies the effect of all other planets, by mixing her good effect with the bad in some, and the good in others, and when too much good is united it sometimes becomes uncontrolable, and a debauched physical body is the result. These combinations will be explained in detail as we proceed with our studies.

MERCURY.

Mercury is the last planet formed in our solar system that can be calculated on, and being very dense and rapid in motion, it has been called the quickener, from the fact, that as Mercury comes into strong aspect to one of the other planets, the effect of that planet seems to be quickened, intensified. The fact is, however, that Mercury's vital and intense vibration, has been added to the effect of the other planet, and the two together form a greater force and influence.

As an illustration, suppose that Saturn has been operating upon the head and brain for several weeks, and has caused a contraction of the arteries and veins, penetrating the brain. When Mercury comes suddenly into Aries, the blood is rapidly forced to the head and brain. The contracted condition retards the blood, and Mercury forces an extra amount, and the result is commotion and distress, and many times death from the bursting of a vessel.

Saturn's influence was not changed by this aspect of Mercury, but the two forces were acting at the same time and could not harmonize. Now, if Venus had come into aspect at the same time that Mercury did, she would have so harmonized and equalized the other two forces, that nothing serious or even very painful would be experienced, so Mercury may be considered simply as a stinger, with great vitality, activity and intensity.

Mercury is the life giver, and rules the inmost principle in physical existence, which is the blood, the entire circulation of which is produced or influenced by his wonderful flight through space.

Mercury being such an active, intense, and vital magnet, is the most expressive and impulsive of them all, therefore expression, vitality, activity, impulse, desire and willingness, are the result in human beings who have Mercury in strong aspect at birth. On account of this the phrenological indications of Mercury are vitality, temper, impulsiveness, expression, speech, sensitiveness and desire.

SUN.

The Sun is the center of the system and being 880,000 miles in diameter, holds this entire group of planets, sattelites, and planetoids, in position through the power of attraction, the law of matter.

As the soul of man is also the center of his system, it too holds the physical structure together and vivifies every molecule which it contains.

The soul of man therefore bears a certain relation to, and must co-ordinate with a certain principle, power, force, or energy expressed in that wondrous Orb. Seek ye the ray that binds your soul to him, and you will find the way that leads to wisdom and power.

RECAPITULATION.

MERCURY rules vitality, the blood, circulation, expression, activity, the five senses, speech, oratory, and executive powers; also temper, sensuality, materiality, and desire.

VENUS governs the affections, and harmonizes the physical organism. Health, love, perception, tune, soul force, satisfaction, appetite and sexual desires, are under the power of Venus.

MARS rules physical force, intellect, parental affection, materiality, anger, combativeness, calculation, mathematical accuracy, the desire to rule, and leadership.

JUPITER controls the muscular system, hence mental power, physical power, individuality, ambition, acquisitiveness, firmness, balance, attraction, locality, time and love of glory, is the result in Jupiter characters.

SATURN creates selfish desires, secretiveness, caution, inharmony, dissatisfaction, disease, distress, failure, and trouble, but gives that quality called tenacity, continuity.

URANUS indicates spiritual powers, veneration, benevolence, energy, endurance, labor, scientific research, genius, invention, honesty, perception, inspiration, clairvoyance, and those qualities which make people Mystical.

NEPTUNE signifies morality, protection, self-esteem, conscience, firmness, comprehension, expansion, stiffness, coldness, love of blood and kind, slow to anger, slow to forgive, steadiness, calmness, travel and change.

The student should commit the foregoing statements of generalities concerning the significance of the planets, before attempting to read or delineate a horoscope of the heavens.

THE MOON being a sattelite of the Earth, and moving around the same apparently every twenty-eight days, must be considered geocentrically. Being formed from a ring thrown off by the earth she partakes of the nature of the Earth, and is constant in effect upon the Earth. But the Earth and Moon together are both effected by the change produced on their entrance into succeeding signs, relative to the Sun. For instance, when the Earth, and of course the Moon, are in Scorpio, the Earth is in the sex function of nature, and as the Moon directly influences generation of every description upon the Earth, when the Moon reaches its opposition aspect to the Sun, or at full Moon, the Moon is also in Scorpio, geocentrically. The effect is to polarize the positive physical forces to the sexual organs. This is the mating season of the year. The season of planting and sowing, which is more intense at full Moon than at any other time during the time the Earth is in that sign.

Many gardners know that they must follow the signs of the Moon if they wish to raise a good crop, so they sow cabbage seed when the Moon is in Aries, if in April, therefore April is the best time to start them, for it is new Moon in Aries at that time that brings the best fruition to all the products of the garden whose positive pole, that is to say, the place where the seed ripens, is in the head of the stalk above the ground. Turnip and beet seed should be sown when the

Moon is in its last quarter polarized to Aquarius or Pisces, in April, because the fruit thereof is developed under the ground or surface of the Earth. Corn, however, should be planted when the Moon is in Libra, in April and May, so that the kernel will be full and plump. The reason is because corn comes to fruition on the body of the stalk.

For best results in raising wheat, it should be sown when it is new Moon in Aries, that is in April, which will polarize the positive pole of the life of the kernel to the head of the stalk, and a full seed will result, whereas, if the Moon is in Libra when seeding is done, there will be a large growth of stalk, and the kernel will not fill, it will be shrunken. These principles apply to all products, vegetable, animal and human.

To illustrate this principle in human life to which this work more particularly applies, if a child is conceived when the Moon is in Aries, the mind will be positive, forceful, intense and clear, so far as the Moon's effects are concerned. But if the Moon be in Libra, the child will be more negative and physical in nature and will have to move its whole body in order to speak, while the other would have the expression on the end of the tongue, and the body could remain quiet while the tongue moved and gave the expression. If the Moon is in Pisces at conception the child when grown will have to walk in order to think clearly.

The Moon is related to the Earth and Sun through the base and perpendicular of the Mystical Triangle, eternal in the Heavens, and to the Sun direct, through the hypotenuse of the same. But this has very little meaning except in spherical trigonometry as applied in geocentric astronomy.

The Moon therefore governs generation and polarization of the positive forces, poles or principles, in physical combinations of every description upon this globe. Character in human life, however, is the result of the combined forces of every planet in our solar system.

AN ERROR.

In order to explain an error which leads many occult astronomers astray concerning the Moon, the following diagram is given to illustrate the effect of the Moon in different signs. When the Earth enters Libra in the month of March the Sun is in Aries, and the relation of the Earth to the Sun is very positive, but physical in nature, in our latitude, and when the Moon is new it too is in Aries, so the attraction is very strong upon the Earth, pulling towards that sign, hence it is the best time for sowing the seeds heretofore mentioned. But in case we wish to do sowing the last of June, if we waited for the Moon to reach the sign Aries it would be in its last quarter, which would be all right for potatoes but a very bad time for wheat.

When the moon reaches the sign Cancer during the month of July the most positive generative effect is produced, and will give the best results from such products as come to fruition in the head as stated, for the influence of the Moon is the result of its relation to the Sun, instead of the signs, therefore the moon will be treated by its phases, in this work instead of by signs. Phases are fixed relations and are constant. Signs are changing every thirty days.

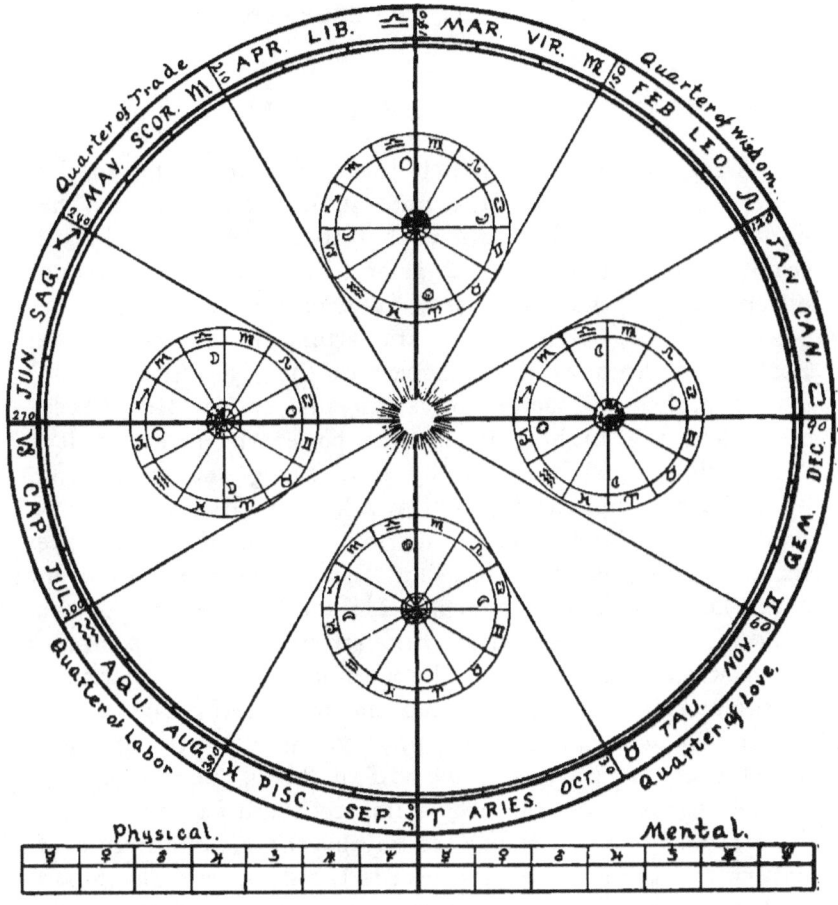

3.

CONCERNING DELINEATION.

After arranging the planets in position according to the tables of positions, for the date under consideration, the figure is ready for delineation ; but to aid the judgment in reading the same, it is best to refer to the physiological and phrenological percentages and fix firmly in the mind the powers of the planets that are strong in aspect to the Earth, also those strong in aspect to the sign Aries. The planet highest in power physically is called the physical ruler; the highest in mental power the mental ruler. The reading must be given by considering the houses the planets are in, not the degrees, for a house is like a platform-scale, when a planet crosses a meridian, it is on the edge of the scale and the effect is weighed in that house, the most even effect, however, is when the planet reaches the center of the house, and is considered slightly stronger in that position, which weakens gradually to the meridian. When a planet is on the meridian the effect is bad, the force being divided between two houses, and many physical disturbances are produced, such as paralysis of one-half the body, one arm or leg, crooked heads, jaws, and bad joints, teeth and features.

If the sign Aries is afflicted say by the cross currents of Saturn and Mars in strong aspect to the same, and the Moon is also polarized to Aries, the positive forces of so many, meeting at the head and such bad influences, causes a commotion in the brain and a serious condition throughout the system. Many marks and disfigurements result from such centralization. Therefore it is very important that these laws by which we are obliged to make our entry into this mortal sphere should be understood.

SOLAR ANATOMY.

Diagram No. 4 illustrates the divisions of the physical man as determined by the solar meridians, each house or sign including a vital section in the anatomy of our being. We are built up physically by the expansion, the vivication of liquid substance, that is to say, the soul, or astral, which comes to be incarnated, re-incarnated, or embodied again, forms a magnetic attachment to this liquid spark from the parent, as a spider would attach its web to an article and drop down or go away from the point of connection, to return to the exact spot with its web at will. As soon as this magnetic relation is fixed and made permanent, the soul or astral vibrates this substance and attracts the best material possible with which to build up a physical body, under the law in operation at the time. This is the reason that women are so sensitive while carrying children, they are vibrated by this spirit who is building a new body in which to gain experience and wisdom under the environment of matter, for it is here in the flesh that souls learn the most valuable lessons and gain the greatest amount of wisdom and power over and concerning material things.

To make the most favorable conditions therefore, for the operations of a soul that seeks to embody, is the law of sex, and to transgress or to interfere with this natural condition, is to interfere with a soul's expression.

A word to the blind has little meaning, but a word to the seeker after wisdom should be sufficient.

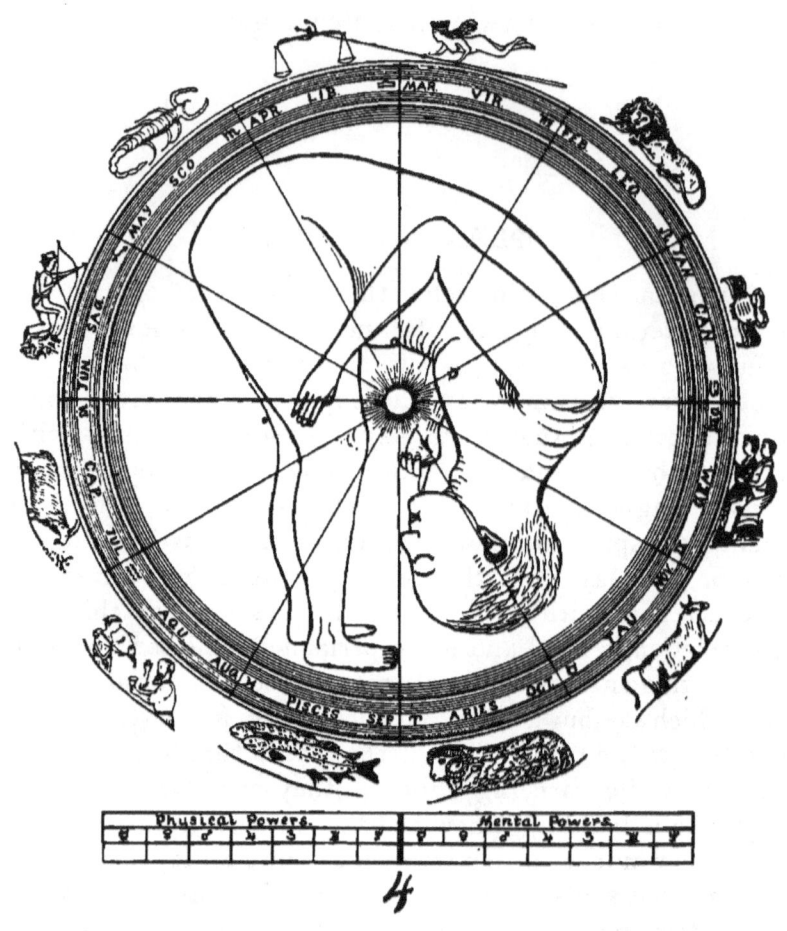

4

SYMBOLISM.

As we turn backward in the history of nations and peoples, we find that many signs, tokens and symbols were once used to express ideas, principles and truths. The signs of the Zodiac have come to us through the ages, and originated so far back that history fails to give us any clue to their origin. But when we begin to look into the philosophy of life and begin to understand something of the law of being, we find the meaning of every symbol that has been used by man, and, to show that this is possible, the following explanation of the signs of the Zodiac, and other symbols, and why they were chosen to represent principles and qualities in man are given.

It must be remembered that the ancients found the principles, laws, functions, and qualities in man before they adopted symbols to express them. They found by observation, association and comparison that persons born in October, or when the Sun had crossed a certain latitudial line, were positive, active in mental pursuits, had intellect, intuition, perception, brain power, expression, and all of the qualities indicated by the sign Aries as hereinbefore stated. They discovered this and to make a record of the fact, was the important duty of the close observer of nature. In looking around they found that the butting ram, that was always banging his head and brain against something, was the most expressive of that positive nature or quality in man, therefore they placed the Ram in that division or section of the solar circle called Aries.

It has been stated that the stars in the constellation Aries were in such a position, and relation, that they actually formed the outlines of a ram. There could be no greater astronomical blunder. The constellations never had anything to do with the origin of the signs of the Zodiac so far as forming the outlines of the characters used.

In like manner they found that Taurus people, that is those born in that season or time of the year, had muscular power, nerve, and a high sex vibration, were somewhat bull-necked, as well as bull-headed, so in looking to nature, for they were naturalists in those days, they found that the bull was the best thing they could select to express vim, muscular strength, nerve, life, force and the qualities heretofore mentioned concerning Taurus, so they very appropriately placed the drawing of a Bull at the sign Taurus.

The lung house Gemini expressive of marriage, unions, quality, in various ways, especially the two lungs, was represented by the Twins, why not? Could there be a more appropriate symbol produced? What we now call cancer was first found in the breast of woman, and when taken out had the appearance of a Crab, which is a fact to-day as too many can testify. Thus the crab was chosen to express the only difficulty people have had and the chief thing that gave people anxiety in that section of their bodies.

Leo being the section of the heart the source of the physical power and life, they chose the Lion, emblematic of power, being the king of the forest, as a symbol to express the heart.

Persons born in Virgo were found to be chaste and pure, hence the Virgin.

Libra men were business men and well balanced harmonious characters, and the Balances were placed as a symbol for that section.

Scorpio characters were found to be strongly sexed, and natural sowers. As the secret organs were included in this section, the Scorpion was decided upon, which if properly handled is harmless and of use, but when abused, stings and poisons. It is not necessary to state the stings that result from the abuse of the sexual functions, and when properly used, the grandest tribute that is possible may be paid to the infinite powers, by making the best physical conditions for the embodiment of a soul.

Sagittarius represents the lower limbs, travel, independence, and a changeable nature. The Archer, which in more modern phraseology is called the rover, or "masher," who is always aiming his darts at the Virgins, aptly represents the character.

The Goat symbolizes labor, hardship, endurance and industry. Also the product of industry—food and raiment.

The Water Bearer represents the most welcome laborer of ancient times, and Aquarius people are the best laborers we have at the present time, hence the symbol of the Water Bearer bringing the water of life.

Pisces being the most negative pole of the solar circle, producing characters that were always active on their feet, and also expressing the law of evolution in physical expression from the negative to the more positive condition as well as the custom and necessary practice of washing the feet, after the travels and labors of the day were finished, they chose two Fishes to symbolically express the two feet and the various traits, customs and principles of Pisces characters, as understood at the time.

The Sphinx is a symbol or record in stone, of the evolution of man from the lower and more negative animal state, to the higher mental and spiritual condition.

The Snake is the most important symbol that has ever been used, or ever will be used upon this globe. When man discovered that there was a law of matter, a law that controlled human organisms, and every function and faculty of their beings; when they discovered that the planets moved under exact direction and power, and when they had arrived at a state of intellectual development, and perception, where they could closely observe and realize the wonderful harmonies of the spheres; they discovered that wonderful operation in nature called in our language, vibration. They found that the finest fibers strung in the air would give forth music when played upon by the breezes, and that the sound was the result of the movement, the undulation, or the vibration that ensued, and by making a close study of the causes of different phenomena they found that everything discoverable by man was in a state of vibration, motion, activity. They found that this vibratory motion like the waves of the ocean was wavelike. That is, there seemed to be no result of moment in the movements of things except when there was a crook or curve or rapid movement back and forth, as best illustrated by a ripple on the water.

Fire illustrated this principle, as well as water and earthly things, and the air seemed to be teeming with this wonderful activity. But probably their own organisms gave them more evidence of this wonderful force, through the emotional and pulsating nature, than they could find elsewhere. They certainly found that the law of the Infinite is vibration, energy, force, activity. Positive and negative in character. They found the wisest men were more active mentally, more intellectual, quicker to perceive and realize the truths expressed in nature, therefore, vibration indicated the degree of intelligence in human beings to a great extent.

After ages of research and study, and the recording in various ways of the facts as learned and exemplified by them through succeeding incarnations; probably many of them counciled together and sought to adopt a symbol that would express this universal principle in nature. Many symbols were no doubt presented, and considered, but after thorough examination, and comparison, they adopted the Snake.

We will not attempt to explain all of the facts in nature they found that the snake aptly symbolized, but will come down to the present time and state a few of the principles apparent to-day.

We find that the snake aptly expresses the positive and negative poles of everything in nature, and when placed around the center, as illustrated in diagram of symbols, shows the meeting of the positive and negative principles in the law of our solar system. As the snake moves along upon the ground it expresses that wavelike motion mentioned, and shows the curves, or lines, of the planets in their onward march through space. For the planets and Moon move in a wavelike path. They never go exactly in a straight line. In short they move as the snake moves. We also find that a snake coils himself around and forms a spiral position, and as he springs forth, he expresses the spiral movements of the planets also. For they not only move in wave lines, but in spiral curves as well.

The snake expresses the renewal of the body, by casting off its old skin and sliding out with a new outfit, which is very emblematic of re-incarnation. The snake has the power to charm other animals, as well as people, which is the gift of mesmerism, or hypnotism. This power which they possess has given them the title of wisdom, the parable, "Be ye wise as serpents, and as harmless as doves," clearly recognizes this quality of wisdom and power in the snake.

It seems to me there is no end to things in nature, that the snake very appropriately symbolizes, therefore it is reason-

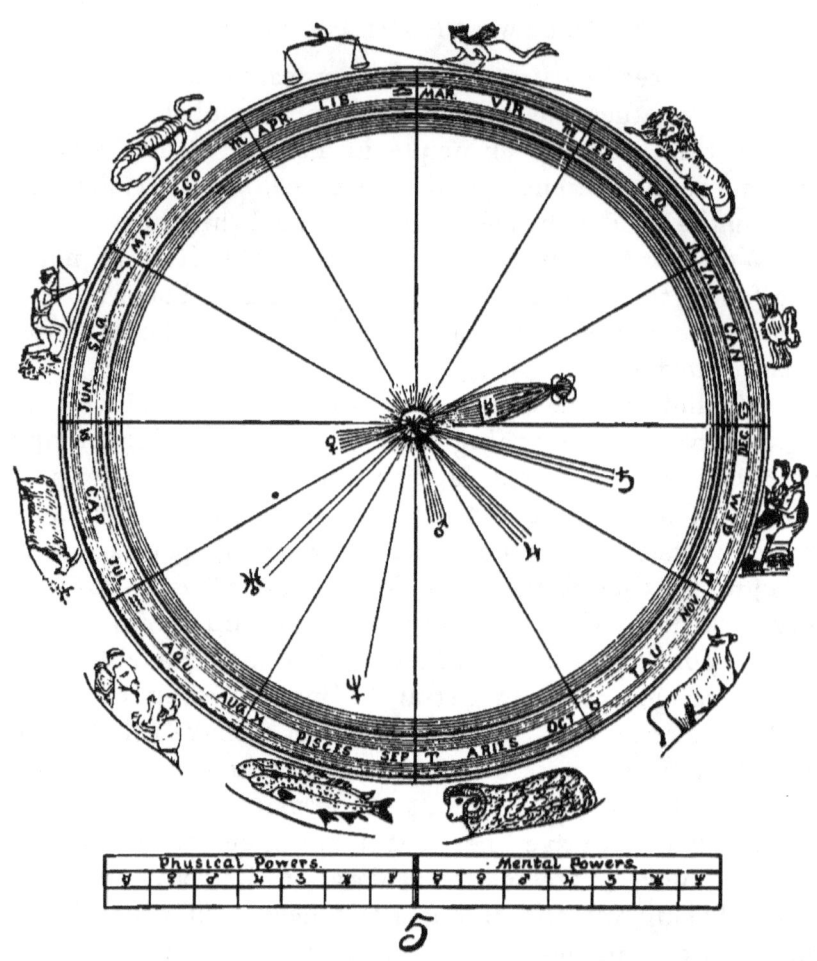

SPECIAL SIGNIFICANCE OF THE PLANETS CONDENSED.

PHYSICAL.		MENTAL.	
☿	Blood and Vitality.	☿	Speech and Wit.
♀	Astral Fluids and Harmony.	♀	Pathos and Rhythm.
♂	Glands and Ducts.	♂	Force and Accuracy.
♃	Muscular System.	♃	Oratory and Rhetoric.
♄	Flesh and Bones.	♄	Logic and Argument.
♅	Brain and Nerves.	♅	Sentiment and Perception.
♆	Skin and Hair.	♆	Firmness and Grandeur.

It is well to commit the above special condensed statements concerning the significance of the different magnets, all of which must be calculated upon in every delineation, in order to reach a satisfactory result.

CONCERNING READINGS.

It has been deemed best to give the lessons teaching the science of reading the Stars, by placing the horoscope of the heavens before the student with the symbols and signs in plain view, in order to more fully impress the mind with the principles to be considered. The first twelve lessons take the Earth into and through the twelve signs, and covers the year 1893, the most important year for many centuries. They show the changes which took place and indications on the dates given.

The next twelve lessons given, are of dates on which Saturn is polarized in each of the twelve signs.

It is intended that these twenty-four lessons will, when thoroughly understood, prepare any one of ordinary intelligence so they may clearly delineate any combination that may be found.

Remember that those who understand Basic Principles best, are the best delineators.

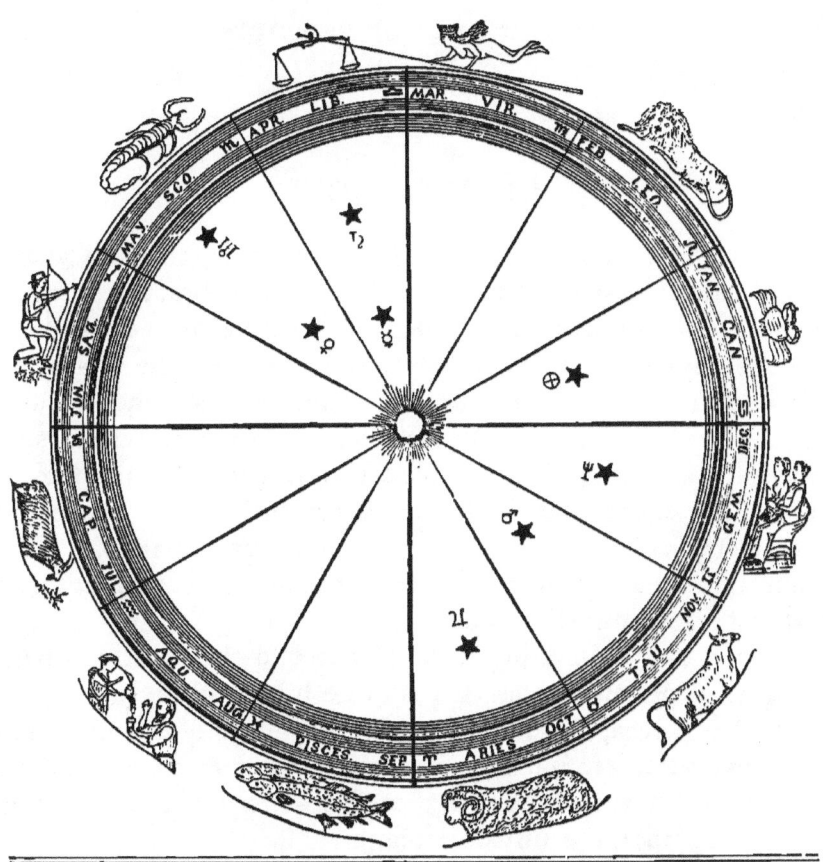

PHYSICAL POWERS.							MENTAL POWERS.					
☿	♀	♂	♃	♄	♅	♆	☿	♀	♂	♃	♄	♅	♆
67	73	73	94	64	61	55	88	52	67	76	64	28	37

DIAGRAM No. 6.

DELINEATION.

January 4th, 1893, the Earth is in Cancer, and as Cancer is in quadratic aspect to the sign Aries, and Libra, the position of the Earth is balanced between the positive or mental sign and the physical or material sign, and shows in the character of a person born at this time a balance between mental and physical extremes, such characters are adapted to pursuits in physical lines, requiring careful study and intelligent perception. The Moon has just passed its full phase, hence the characteristics of the sign Cancer are very marked. The Earth is poised here to receive from the other planets, and the first to be considered is Mercury.

MERCURY is in Libra in fifth aspect to the Earth, at 67% of physical power, and as this is quite high and in the physical sign of Libra, the effect is largely material, and materialistic tendencies are indicated. This is Mercury's single effect. The vibrant force of Mercury causes sensitiveness, but it is manifested upon the physical plane.

VENUS is the second planet, and is polarized in Scorpio in conjunction with Uranus in first or weakest aspect to the Earth, at 73% of physical power, which, being low for Venus, shows that the person born at this time will have very little affection, owing to the weak aspect, and what they do have will be universal. They will never worship any one person. They will not express tenderness and sympathy readily and naturally, hence they will be considered cold and unsympathetic. The mental effect is weaker still, only 52%, therefore the speech will be blunt and somewhat harsh, being under the influence of Mercury, Jupiter and Saturn, which are in strong aspect to Aries, the sign of speech and expression.

The physical effect of Venus is very good even at her low percentage and weak aspect to the earth, for she is in fifth aspect to Leo the heart, and in sixth, or opposition aspect to the sign Taurus, which section includes the nerve and muscular centers, thus softening and harmonizing the nervous system, which Mars and Uranus are disturbing to some extent.

MARS being in Taurus fires up the blood and causes antagonistic feelings to appear. This is on account of Mars being in strong aspect, fifth to Leo, which rules the heart and blood. Whenever Mars is vibrating upon the heart at birth this stamp of Mars is placed there for the entire earthly career, and whenever Mars comes into aspect to this sign, especially when to the same position as at birth, the person thus stamped, will have these combative Mars feelings greatly intensified.

As mentioned before Venus softens up the Mars effect by counteracting his bad vibrations with her exceedingly good ones, equalizing the two, which means that this person, or a person born under this horoscope, will not be severe or to any great extent combative.

JUPITER is in Aries at 77% of physical power upon the Earth, and as Jupiter is a powerful magnet, he draws everything toward the sign he is in. Hence people generally, will turn to the mental, the spiritual and intellectual, affairs in life, when Jupiter is in this sign, and seek to gain wisdom, more particularly than wealth. Those born under this combination of forces will be intellectual, and although Jupiter rules them strong, they will not become money makers to any great degree, although they will be able to make all and more than they need. The mental percentage of Jupiter is 76% which is quite high, and indicates great mental strength and power. Mercury in opposition at 88% of mental force, makes a strong combination for oratorical achievements. Jupiter is physical and Mercury is mental ruler, which indicates strength and power both physically and mentally.

SATURN is in the physical center, and is 64% in physical and also 64% in mental strength, which indicates that Saturn is a very powerful magnet to be considered in this combination. Jupiter has the tendency to draw people away from business into intellectual studies and pursuits, while Saturn is acting just the opposite, and is drawing people under him, into the business world. On account of this, there are many Saturn characters becoming leaders and directors in business, and political affairs, and as Saturn characters are not good business magnets, from the time Saturn enters the physical or trade center until he passes out again, there must necessarily be trouble and commotion in the business world. A person born under this combination is not fitted for business because of Saturn's high percentage and position.

Saturn, however, is balanced by Jupiter in mental power, and Mercury, the giver of speech is in conjunction, which shows us that this is an excellent combination for a lawyer, a politician and a leader, to be born under. Therefore, in stating where such characters belong, and what they should prepare for, I would advise the legal profession, with a view of entering the political arena, for the greatest glory.

URANUS is very low in both physical and mental power, which shows us that these characters will not be religious ones to any great degree. It shows us also, that they will not work in a physical way, but will get through the world bossing others, for Uranus people are workers.

NEPTUNE is weak and has very little bearing upon this

combination. When Neptune passed into Gemini in 1889 pneumonia, la grippe and lung difficulties, were intensified by his cold, damp, phlegmatic effect, and when Saturn reached the fifth aspect, in the house of Virgo, in 1890 the combination of Saturn and Neptune on the stomach and lungs, culminated the lives of a great many people. Especially was it noticeable among those who were fleshy, robust, and high livers. Their stomachs being weak from high living, made them yield under this combination, which produced what is called the " Grippe."

DISEASES.

The physical difficulties which this combination will produce in children born at this time, are so slight that it will not be necessary to mention them, except briefly.

The Earth being in Cancer is in a strong house, both physically and mentally. Saturn, the planet that disorganizes the flesh, is balanced by Jupiter. Uranus and Mars are harmonized by Venus, so the forces are evenly balanced. Hence harmony and health will be the result. Slight fevers and an occasional bowel difficulty will come on when Saturn and Mercury are in aspect to Aries, with Jupiter weak in position and aspect.

The stomach is operated on by Neptune in fifth aspect, which indicates a coldness and a somewhat phlegmatic condition, and as like attracts like, cold drinks are better than hot ones in the case of a cold settling in these parts.

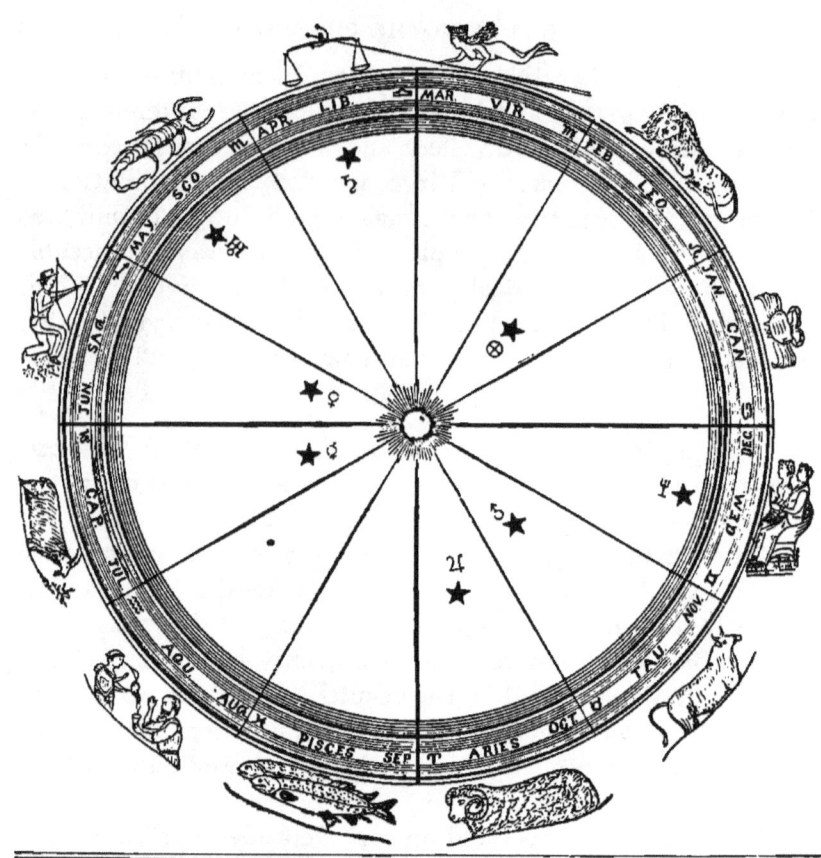

PHYSICAL POWERS.							MENTAL POWERS.					
☿	♀	♂	♃	♄	♅	♆	☿	♀	♂	♃	♄	♅	♆
48	69	75	81	63	72	57	74	74	68	62	59	83	38

DIAGRAM No. 7.

DELINEATION.

February 4th, 1893, we find the Earth in Leo, the house of the heart, and as Mars, the combative and firey planet, and Uranus, the nerve planet, are in opposition, and in fifth position, or quadrature, to the sign Leo and Earth, the heart is highly vibrated, causing rapid circulation of the blood, and rapid manufacture of blood and nerve fluids, which cause these natures very high and acute sensations, in parts ruled by Taurus and Scorpio, which by reflex action afflicts the brain. But as Jupiter is still in Aries no serious brain difficulty need be brought on. Environment, however, may do so.

Knowledge of these things gives power to prevent trouble. The physical strength produced by Jupiter and Saturn is about the same as in previous reading, Saturn having increased slightly while Jupiter has weakened.

Mercury is very low, only 48%, which indicates that this person is vitally weak, and cannot endure physical labor without great fatigue. Venus is 69% and in first position, in opposition to Neptune, and the two in quadrature to the house of Virgo. Virgo being the house of virtue, Venus of love, and Neptune of moral power at 57%, which is high for that planet, shows the moral qualities to be very strong in such natures. As the vitality of this combination is very low, physical labor should not be attempted. Care must be taken of the system to keep up the strength.

DISEASES.

Hysteria and nervous prostration are indicated, owing to the low vitality and the high nervous and firey combination of

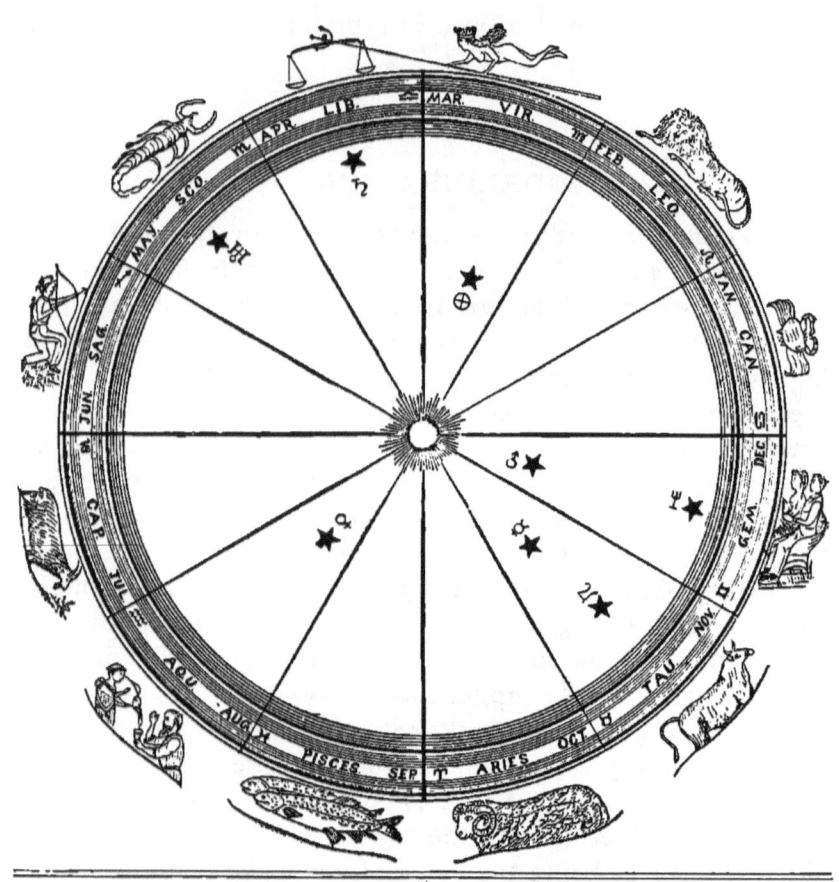

PHYSICAL POWERS.								MENTAL POWERS.						
☿	♀	♂	♃	♄	♅	♆	☿	♀	♂	♃	♄	♅	♆
81	66	69	75	57	69	60	69	48	66	51	57	36	42

DIAGRAM No. 8.

DELINEATION.

March 6th, 1893, the Earth is in Virgo, the house of virtue, wisdom and spirituality, which indicates this kind of a character, as will be seen by Mars, the planet of intellect and power, and Neptune, the magnet giving moral strength, being in quadrature or fifth position to Virgo. Mars and Nuptune are joint rulers in this life. Venus is weak in aspect. Mars being strong in aspect is the mental ruler. Mercury is giving a high expression of vitality to this combination. Jupiter is 75% in Taurus, and strengthens and steadies the nervous system. Saturn is weak, but as Jupiter is now out of opposition, Saturn's effect is not modified in the least. Therefore, these natures vibrate low in the head and brain; also in the bowels, the two conditions so easily affected through, and by the condition of the stomach. Uranus balances Jupiter, and the nervous system is with a fair balance. Neptune at 60% in fifth position, or aspect, gives to such natures a strong desire to travel, and as Mars is the god of war, these characters will be desirous of becoming sea captains, officers, or government representatives of some degree.

Mercury is the physical ruler.

DISEASES.

Bowel difficulties are indicated by Saturn's position, pneumonia, by Neptune's strong effect upon the lung section, while Saturn also effects the sign Cancer, causing low circulation and action in the chest, and by opposition to Aries, the retarded condition in the head. Neuralgia will trouble to some extent as a natural result, produced mostly, however, by the manner of life, and habits of diet.

BUSINESS QUALIFICATIONS.

These characters would make good seamen, fair commanders, good soldiers. They will be natural rovers, and travelers; they will prefer water to land. Military and marine affairs are the most interesting to this class of minds. They will be energetic, as is indicated by Mercury, in the house of energy, Taurus, the nerve and muscular section.

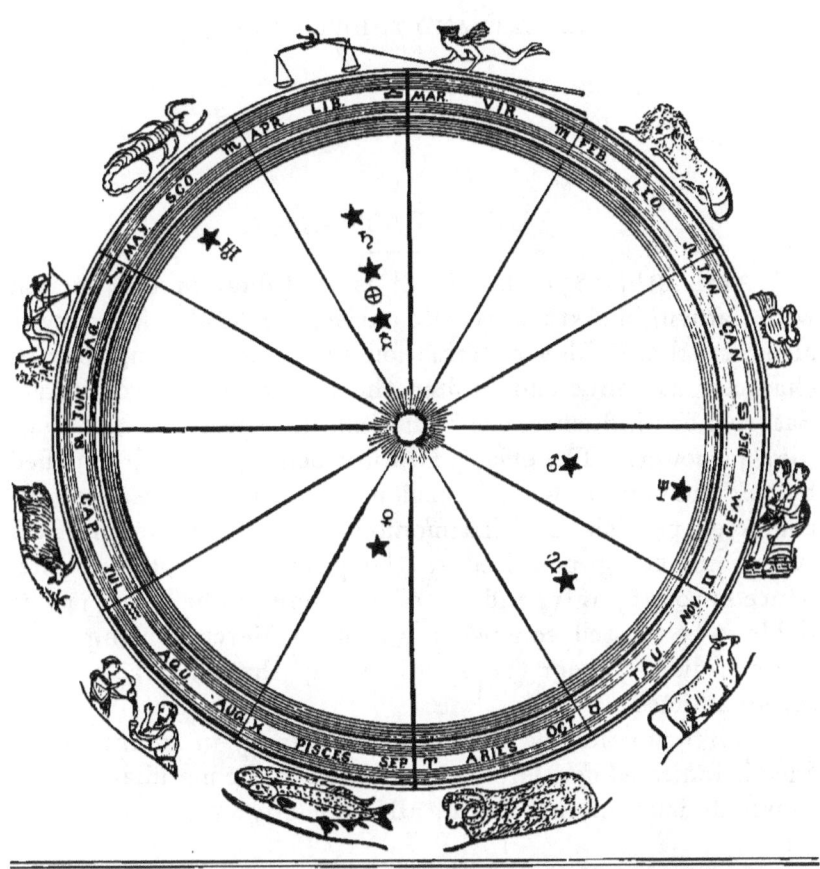

PHYSICAL POWERS.							MENTAL POWERS.						
☿	♀	♂	♃	♄	♅	♆	☿	♀	♂	♃	♄	♅	♆
70	67	55	76	67	64	46	92	44	53	53	68	32	29

DIAGRAM No. 9.

DELINEATION.

April 4th, 1893, the Earth is in Libra, in conjunction with Saturn, in sixth aspect to Aries, the head. Mercury is also in Libra. This combination indicates a strong Saturn character, as Venus and Jupiter, the magnets which counteract Saturn's bad influence, are both weak in aspect, and not very high in power. The effect of Saturn being greatly intensified by Mercury, indicates a tenacious, selfish, and disagreeable character, peevish and inharmonious. Saturn is the physical ruler, and being polarized to the physiognomy, the countenance is rough, ugly, and out of harmony. The lower jaw is liable to be twisted somewhat, owing to Mercury being near the meridian. From the shoulders up these characters are sorely afflicted.

Mercury rules the speech, but hesitancy in giving utterance is indicated by Mercury's nearness to the meridian, which causes division in expression, allowing only a part to be given forth.

Jupiter and Uranus keep the nervous system in fair condition and balance. Mars and Neptune effect the lungs, but as Venus is in quadrature, and harmonizes the combination, it is not very bad. These natures cannot be affectionate owing to Venus being weak in aspect and position.

This is really an inharmonious combination of forces with which to charge a human magnet, but these conditions are for us to meet, and with knowledge of them, and that alone, can we win the battle.

DISEASES.

Fevers, constipation, head difficulties, weak eyes, deafness, and general complaints of this kind will be experienced by these natures. The Moon just passed its full phase, indicates inward suffering, as well as bad outward appearance.

BUSINESS QUALIFICATIONS.

These characters are not fitted for business life, and must necessarily labor for a living. Some agricultural pursuit is best. The salt industry would interest them, as Saturn natures harmonize best with the salt of the Earth. Mining, and handling ores, would also be a desirable business for such magnets. Brain fever, or something more sudden will no doubt culminate these lives.

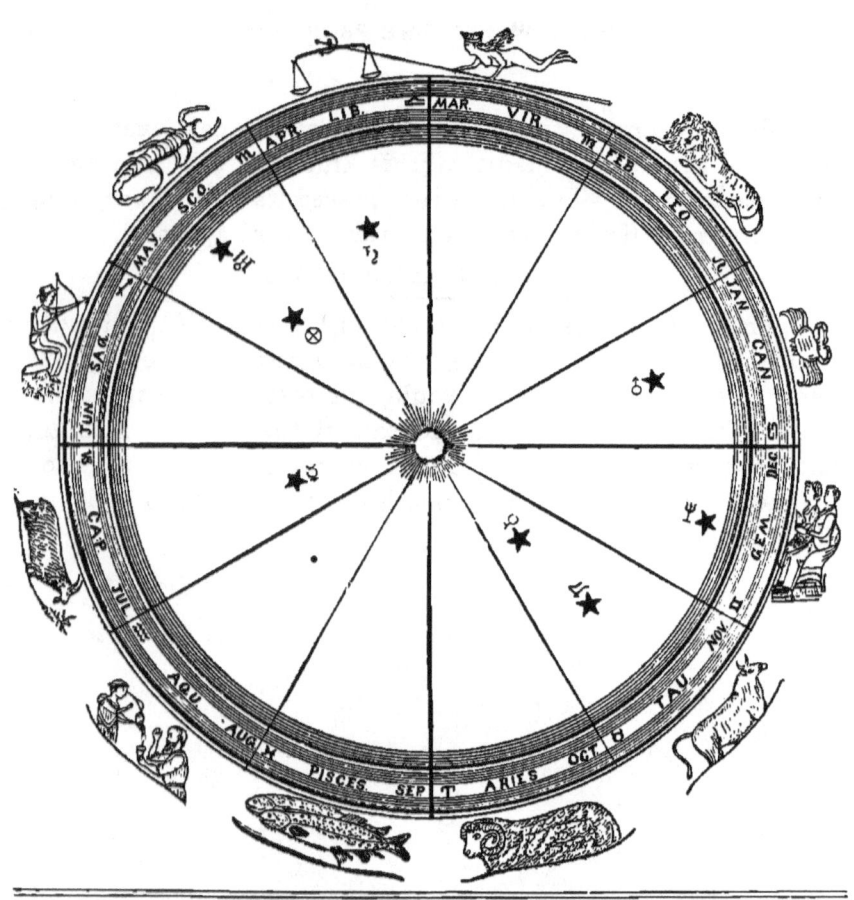

PHYSICAL POWERS.							MENTAL POWERS.						
☿	♀	♂	♃	♄	♅	♆	☿	♀	♂	♃	♄	♅	♆
51	84	48	87	54	75	48	78	78	63	66	54	42	30

DIAGRAM No. 10.

DELINEATION.

May 1st, 1893, the World's Columbian Exposition was opened. We find the Earth in Scorpio, in conjunction with Uranus. Venus and Jupiter are in opposition with Mercury in sextile or fifth position. Jupiter is the physical ruler at 87%, Venus second at 84% and Uranus 75%, all very high, and all three in harmony. Being in the house of, and aspecting Taurus, the nervous system, shows conclusively a well balanced physical structure. Mercury being in sextile to the Earth, and in quadrature to Aries, and in opposition to Mars, indicates a person capable of expressing ideas clearly and intelligently. As Saturn is also in opposition to Aries, and in quadratic aspect to both Mercury and Mars, we have a very strong combination of positions, and aspects. These characters, therefore, are very well proportioned for physical expression, warm and affectionate, with very strong and forcible mental and intellectual tendencies. Neptune influences this date very little.

Observe the difference between the indications in this and the previous reading. Thirty days making excellent magnetic combinations for human expression.

DISEASES

Very high and conflicting vibrations in the brain, and the bowel difficulty, mentioned in former reading, are indicated, but the other physical effects are so favorable that no serious results need follow any attacks that may be experienced.

BUSINESS QUALIFICATIONS.

These characters are adapted to the professions. The ministry, legal profession, medical profession, or the lecture field is best. Why? Because Uranus gives spirituality, Venus gives sympathy, Jupiter power. The Earth is between spirituality and power, money, with Venus to soften the qualities necessary to a Jupiter or money making character. In other words, Uranus—labor, is in opposition to Jupiter—capitol, while Saturn, Mars and Mercury, give intellectual power, and ability to use the same.

They could make their best mark probably in law, as Mars and Saturn give powerful argumentative capabilities. The ministry is next, the lecture field next. Great wealth will never come to such persons through personal efforts, for Uranus will incline the mind more to the intellectual and scientific pursuits, and work will be the result.

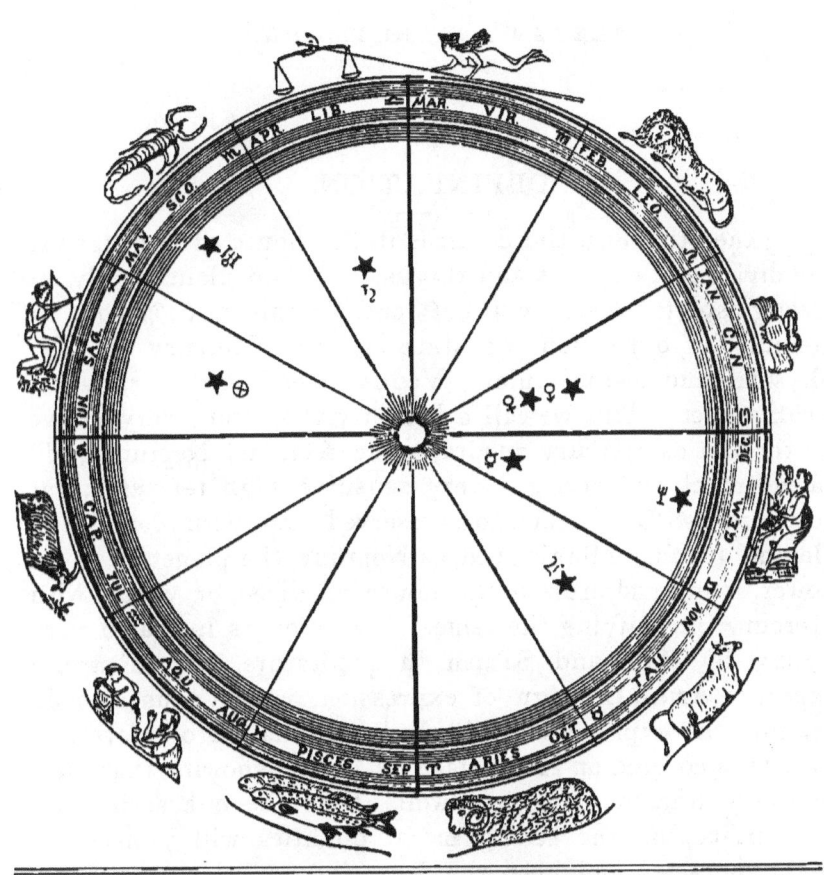

PHYSICAL POWERS.							MENTAL POWERS.						
☿	♀	♂	♃	♄	♅	♆	☿	♀	♂	♃	♄	♅	♆
92	77	50	74	56	62	62	80	71	65	50	56	29	44

DIAGRAM No. 11.

DELINEATION.

June 6th, 1893, the Earth is in the house of Sagittarius, the division of the hips and thighs, with two planets only in strong aspect. Mercury at 92% and Neptune at 62% both in Gemini in opposition, or sixth aspect. Mercury is both physical and mental ruler. Venus second in power, but in weak aspect. This we call a Mercury character; very active on the feet as Mercury quadrates the feet, and Neptune indicates travel and change; very sensitive, high tempered, but cold and stiff in demeanor, reserved and with damp and clammy touch. Morals good, as Neptune, the planet of moral power, is in quadrature to the house of Virgo, or virtue, with Mercury intensifying the same. Deception is indicated very strong by Mars and Saturn in quadrature, and in strong aspect to Aries, the sign of expression, with Venus also directing the expression. The bad combination of Mars and Saturn is covered on the surface by Venus, showing that within a very different character dwells, than the one seen upon the surface, but the strong moral qualities will protect the inner character, and keep the deceptive qualities from being discovered by general acquaintances, and only those with psychometric powers, will be able to read between the lines. Jupiter and Uranus strengthen the physical system as in the previous delineation.

DISEASES.

Paralysis, rheumatism, lumbago, gout, cramps, chills and fever, colds, and damp, cold feet, will afflict these characters, as the result of Mercury, the planet of fevers, being in conjunction with Neptune, the planet of dampness and chills, both in the house of the lungs, in quadrature to the house of Pisces, the feet.

BUSINESS QUALIFICATIONS.

These persons are natural actors, and imitators, as indicated by Mars, Saturn and Venus, aspecting the sign Aries, the sign of expression, indicating double characters, or the ability and inclination to be one faced to the world but another person, in fact. Ingenuity to do this, qualifies one to imitate and personify, and Neptune will be gratified by the traveling and change necessary to a life upon the stage.

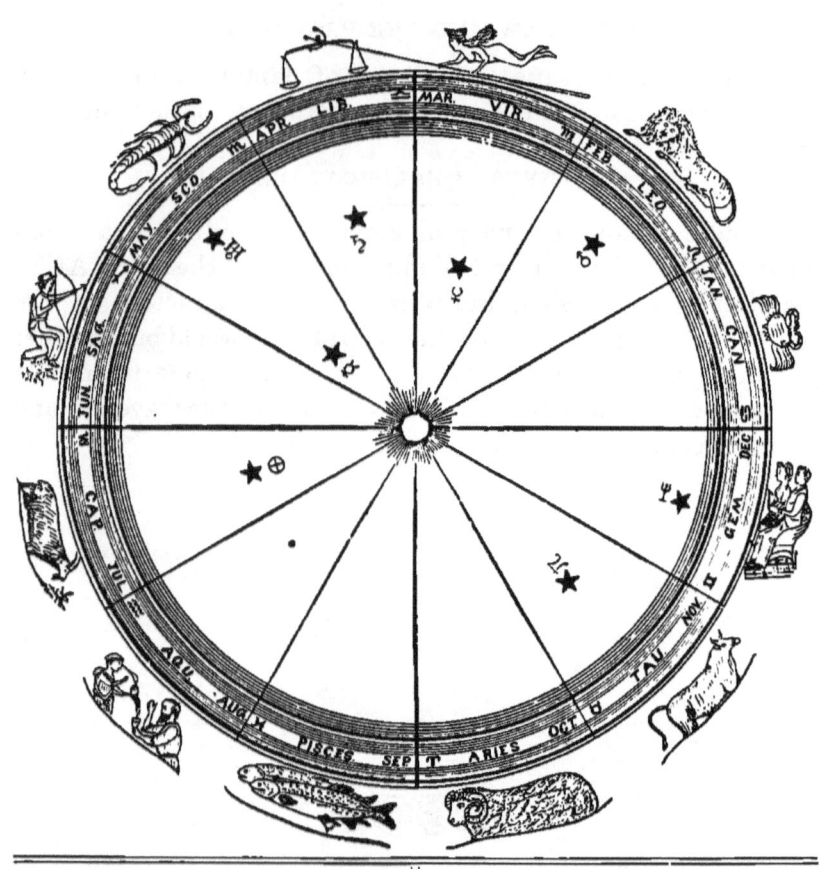

PHYSICAL POWERS.								MENTAL POWERS.						
☿	♀	♂	♃	♄	♅	♆	☿	♀	♂	♃	♄	♅	♆
49	73	43	70	58	64	46	64	52	52	49	61	34	31

DIAGRAM No. 12.

DELINEATION.

July 9th, 1893, we find the Earth alone in the house of the thighs, and limbs, in quadratic aspect to the signs Aries and Libra, with Saturn in Libra, the only planet in strong aspect. This is a strong Saturn character producer, as Mars afflicts the heart house, and fires up the blood. Mercury in conjunction with Uranus, in opposition to Jupiter in the house of energy, nerve, and power, with Venus out of aspect, the combination indicates an inharmonious, irritable and quarrelsome nature. Such persons should live in the country and engage in light farming, where very little responsibility and worry will be known. Mercury at only 49% with Mars at 43%, shows that this is best. Venus being ruler, but weak in aspect shows that this person will not harmonize with people and remain peaceful long.

DISEASES.

Nervous diseases are indicated most on account of Mars afflicting the blood, and Saturn afflicting the brain, with Mercury and Uranus intensifying the nervous system. Jupiter alone keeps such persons from becoming nervous wrecks, but in spite of Jupiter, nervous disorders will trouble them much, and the nervous system must be treated when these natural conditions are aggravated, in order to produce beneficial results.

BUSINESS QUALIFICATIONS.

These characters have no business qualifications worth mentioning, and agricultural pursuits are best, although hard physical labor cannot be endured. But out door life and country life would be best for such people.

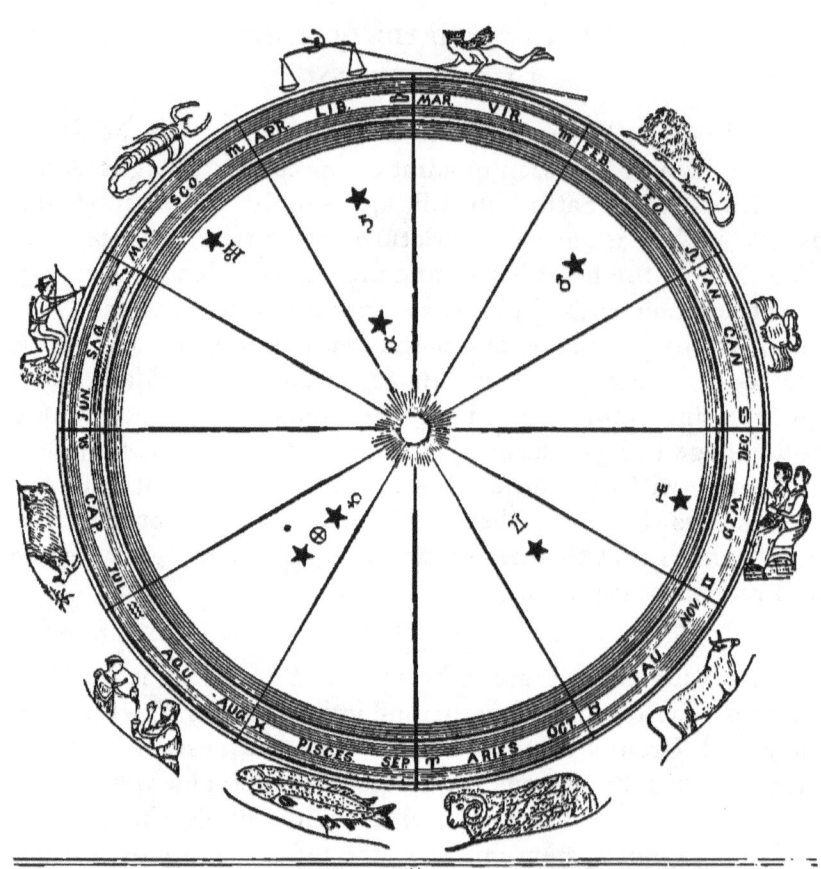

PHYSICAL POWERS.							MENTAL POWERS.						
☿	♀	♂	♃	♄	♅	♆	☿	♀	♂	♃	♄	♅	♆
68	71	56	83	47	68	44	64	64	61	58	46	37	25

DIAGRAM No. 13.

DELINEATION.

August 10th, 1893, the Earth is in Aquarius in conjunction with Mercury, with Mars in Leo, Jupiter in Taurus, Uranus in Scorpio, Saturn and Venus in Libra. Neptune is out of aspect in Gemini. Observe the striking change which has taken place since the last delineation of thirty days ago. Mercury is now 68%, giving high vitality and activity. Jupiter is ruler at 83%. This combination shows us a character with great vital physical power, capable of great endurance, a worker, a pusher in business, a natural contractor, manager, and builder, capable of handling large and extensive deals in contract work. This is the result of the striking balance of physical or magnetic effects of the planets. Mercury and the Earth, in opposition to Mars and Uranus, in opposition to Jupiter, all high in power, while Saturn is low in power, and Venus is in conjunction to soften and harmonize the expression, as well as keeping the head, bowels and physical health generally, in very good condition. Mars is still in Leo, and fires up the blood somewhat, but it is necessary in the business for which these characters are best adapted. Venus will cause them to speak kindly, although within the fire may be raging. These characters rule, always rule.

DISEASES.

Venus being in the sixth position to Aries, shows us that these subjects have very good appetites, and through the gratification of the appetite may become mentally deranged. Mars, Uranus and Mercury, in their present positions, aspecting Leo, the blood; Scorpio, the secrets; Mercury and the

Earth in second aspect to one, and third aspect to the other, make a combined force upon the Earth very powerful. Secret disorders, therefore, are indicated, but generally speaking, these characters must die of old age, as diseases are mild with such a combination of forces.

BUSINESS QUALIFICATIONS.

The characters produced under this combination, will be natural mechanics, mathematicians, and practical jobbers, well adapted to ship building, and large construction work generally. They will make good government contractors. Females of this class are good managers in manufacturing establishments, and will do well in business for themselves. Great wealth cannot be made, however, as Uranus is in opposition to Jupiter, and Mars has a bad effect also upon Jupiter's money making forces.

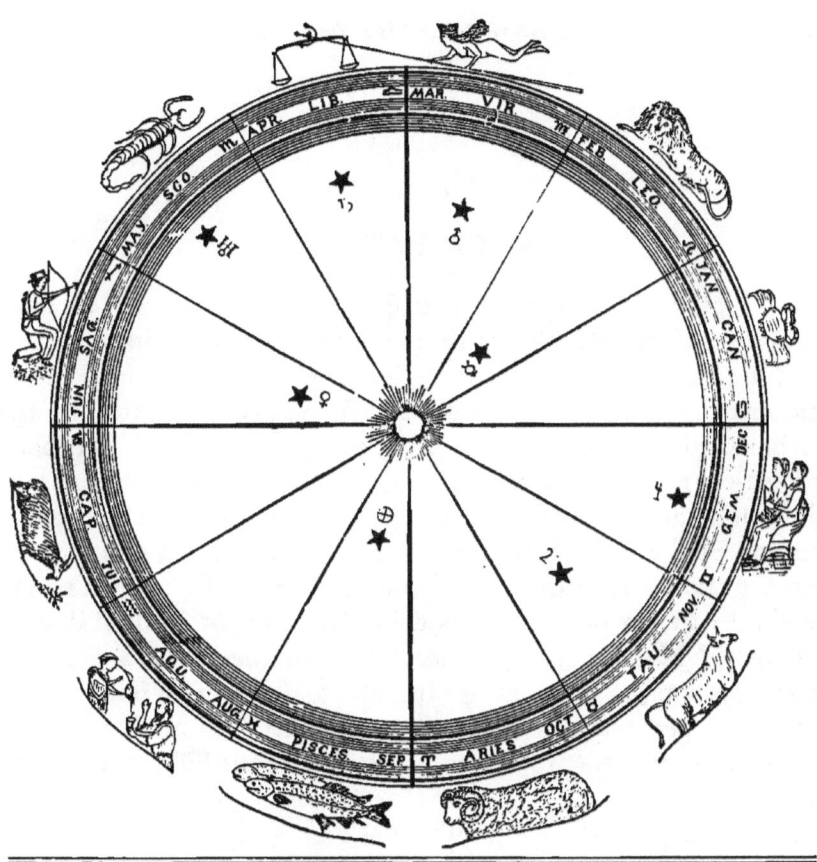

PHYSICAL POWERS.							MENTAL POWERS.					
☿	♀	♂	♃	♄	♅	♆	☿	♀	♂	♃	♄	♅	♆
71	77	50	80	50	56	56	61	55	58	55	49	22	37

DIAGRAM No. 14.

DELINEATION.

September 10th, 1893, the Earth is in Pisces, in opposition to Mars with Venus in quadrature. Jupiter in Taurus, is the physical ruler at 80%. Neptune is also in quadrature in opposition to Venus. Mars and Venus two opposites, make a harmonious average, and in this case give a very well balanced character. Neptune causes a desire to travel, Saturn is left alone and the bad influence is freed again in this combination by Venus. Mercury, Uranus and Jupiter, are in strong aspect and give physical endurance and long life. Mercury is mental ruler, which indicates mentality and intellectual development. Mars in strong aspect shows mathematical accuracy, and systematic reasoning in all matters material. The spiritual perception is not very high, Uranus at 27% only, does not indicate a very clear perception of the hidden forces in nature.

DISEASES.

No serious difficulties are indicated, as Venus is so high in power and there being three opposition aspects, with planets in seven houses, which divides up the forces and equalizes conditions. The head will feel the low vibration of Saturn, and the bowels are still afflicted, but not seriously, as Venus is in sextile to Saturn. The Moon is new and the effect is religious, as the positive physical center of expression is in the head and as Virgo is in strong aspect, the tendency is to the ideal, the religious.

BUSINESS QUALIFICATIONS.

The medical profession is first for these persons, and law is also suited to the character. Mars and Venus make a good combination for the medical practice. Mars is good for law and Saturn assists by aspecting the head, and Jupiter is mentally suited to such work. They will naturally turn to these lines if environment permits.

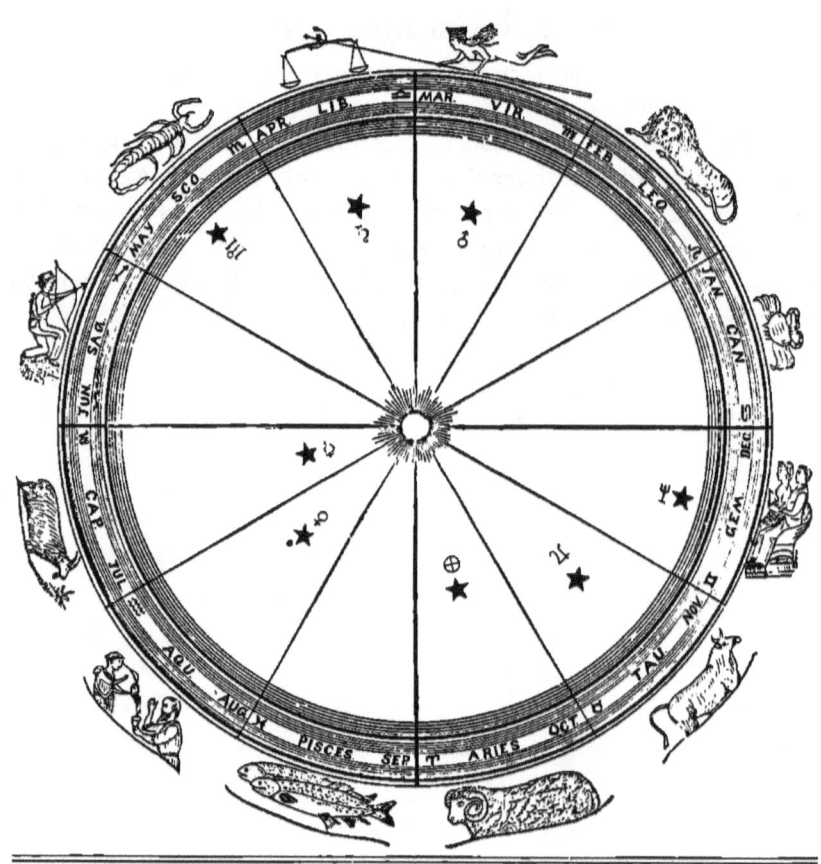

PHYSICAL POWERS.							MENTAL POWERS.						
☿	♀	♂	♃	♄	♅	♆	☿	♀	♂	♃	♄	♅	♆
55	70	40	79	64	61	55	85	55	52	58	67	31	40

DIAGRAM No. 15.

DELINEATION.

October 10th, 1893, the Earth is in Aries, the sign of the head, the most positive position in relation to the Sun that is possible. Saturn is in opposition, and as Mercury is in quadrature to the Earth and Saturn, the effect of Saturn is made dangerous, by the meeting of the two extremes, polarized, or aspected to the head. Mercury indicates fevers, Saturn low vibration, depression, inharmony and rashness. The combination means a character that is very impulsive, tenacious, and subject to violence. Venus in quadrature to Uranus and Jupiter, harmonizes the physical conditions to quite an extent. Neptune in sextile to Aries and the Earth signifies changes, and a desire to investigate new inventions and improvements. Mars is only 40% in physical power, so the combative element is weak. The mental effect of Uranus is very low, which means that the spiritual perception is limited. Mercury, Jupiter, and Saturn, are the mental indicators.

DISEASES.

The Earth being in Aries, the house of the head, the sign of fire, fevers, and high vibration generally, and being aspected by Saturn and Mercury, indicates head difficulties, bowel complaints, especially inflammations. Mercury shows rapid action, while Saturn indicates stricture, the two being antagonistic in nature. The sign Cancer is also weakened, causing inharmony in the chest. The blood is very liable to become thickened by bowel difficulties, and from lack of circulation and power to throw off the impurities through the natural channels. The other weak portions of the system are apt to catch the impure blood, for when it is thick, and clotted it lodges where the circulation is slow. In this case it is the chest, therefore, these characters are liable to cancer of the breast, especially females, unless they keep their systems free from pollution.

In case one should consult this system of diagnosing diseases, it will be safe to conclude, from the positions under consideration, that as the circulation is very much afflicted, and the system is one with feverish tendencies, cancer must necessarily result if it be a lady, and thirty or thirty-five years of age. If a man, brain fever, loss of memory, and bewilderment in the head generally. The reason women are afflicted more with cancer is on account of the corset, which most of them wear. The corset retards the circulation about the chest, intensifying the natural weakness in that section.

BUSINESS QUALIFICATIONS.

Quickness, and rashness, unfits these characters for business. Agricultural and mining pursuits would suit such natures best. The minerals and salts of the Earth co-ordinate with these conditions, and the roughness of such life, meets the rashness of the nature of those born under such a magnetic combination.

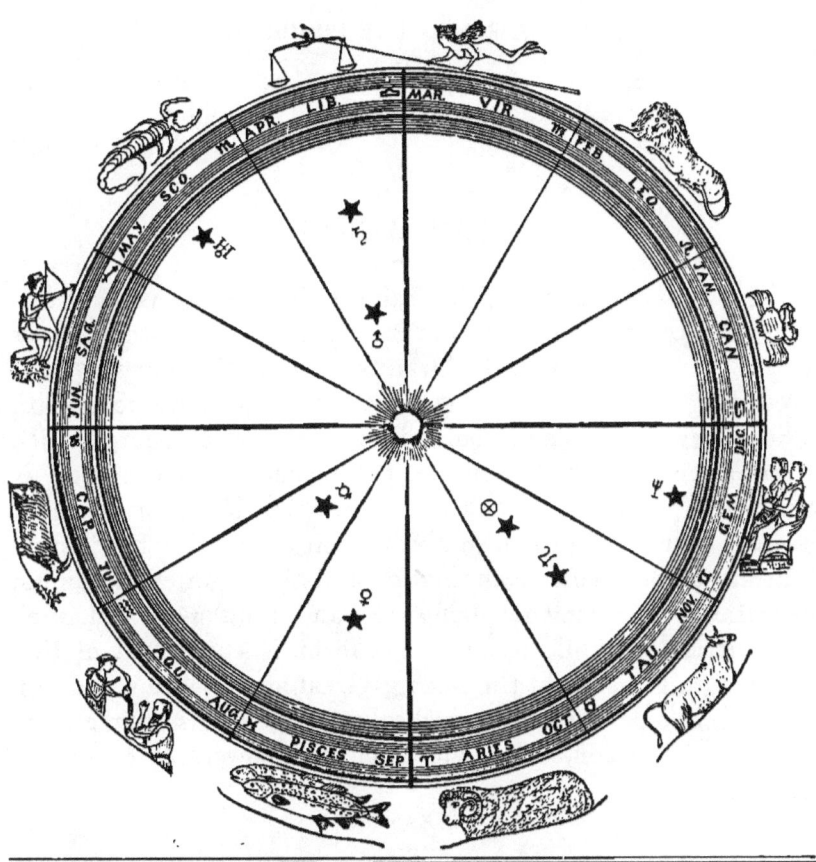

PHYSICAL POWERS.							MENTAL POWERS.						
☿	♀	♂	♃	♄	♅	♆	☿	♀	♂	♃	♄	♅	♆
65	74	47	92	53	74	53	60	48	63	66	51	39	33

DIAGRAM No. 16.

DELINEATION.

November 7th, 1893, the Earth is in Taurus, in conjunction with Jupiter, with Uranus in opposition. Jupiter is ruler at 92%, Venus is at 74%, Uranus at 74%, Mercury at 65%, producing great physical strength, and capacity for labor. These characters being born in the house of energy, with Jupiter, the planet of muscle, power and wealth, shows us characters capable of making money by labor or contract work. Mars and Saturn in sixth position to the head sign, indicate a bad mental combination and the countenance must necessarily be somewhat disfigured and repulsive from such conjunction. Crankiness in some form, is the result of this relation, to the sign of the head. Great mental strain and self-condemnation from no outward cause, afflicts this character as a result of the combative and tenacious powers of these two magnets.

DISEASES.

Uranus, the planet of the nervous system, and Mercury, the planet of fevers and high vibration, being very strong in these characters, show that a bad condition of the brain, caused by the conjunction of Mars and Saturn, means head difficulty, bordering on insanity. Jupiter gives physical strength and endurance but is acting upon the muscular system, principally, making these dangerous characters to oppose. The mind and nervous system is afflicted in this case and all other indications are trivial.

BUSINESS QUALIFICATIONS.

These natures are adapted to the slaughtering business, stock, and packing house pursuits, where vent may be given to the natural, intense emotions, from within. Two conditions that are congenial result in harmony, hence the above judgment.

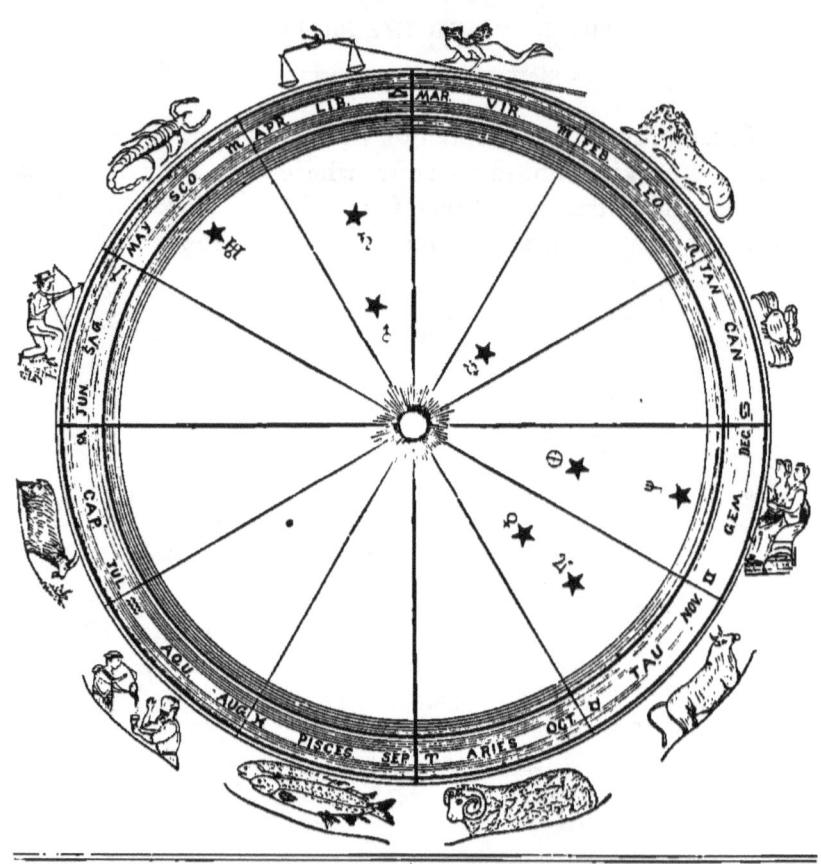

PHYSICAL POWERS.							MENTAL POWERS.					
☿	♀	♂	♃	♄	♅	♆	☿	♀	♂	♃	♄	♅	♆
81	77	45	81	51	63	66	70	67	61	55	49	28	46

DIAGRAM No. 17.

DELINEATION.

December 7th, 1893, the Earth is in conjunction with Neptune, the planet of travel, commerce, change, and enlargement. Gemini is the house of the lungs, and Neptune being a wet, cold, damp, influence, and so strong upon the Earth with no aspect of other counteracting influences, reveals a very strong Neptune character, a natural rover, a person of high moral character, but cold, distant and reserved. Jupiter is physical ruler, and is in position to steady the nervous system. Mars and Saturn still afflict the head, but Mercury, the ruler of the blood, is in Leo, and gives rapid circulation. This, with a natural Neptunian organism, averages up and gives a fair physical condition, generally speaking. This person will have a cold hand shake, cold feet, and a rather stiff demeanor. The character is marked and intensely individual, as there are three conjunctions and two quadratures in the expression, which always indicate marked and powerful characteristics.

DISEASES.

Colds, and stiffness in joints, chills and fever, will result from two conditions in the system, Neptune causing a cold, damp state, and Mars and Saturn and Mercury, a hot and agitated condition.

BUSINESS QUALIFICATIONS.

Persons of this nature are natural seamen, and are adapted to a business which extends over the seas. Any large coast trade, or the fishing industry is suited to these characters.

The foregoing twelve readings are given, to explain in a general way, the method of procedure in considering the positions and relations for any given date, but in writing the Law of Being, for a person, a certain form should be used, which will give the special characteristics in clear and definite terms, explain the reasons for the conclusions, and also state what the primal causes of physical disorders are, and also explain the method and formula for relief, and restoration to a harmonious and natural condition under the law. And if need be, to show how to rise superior to the physical law, in case bad and inharmonious magnetic conditions are natural.

DIAGNOSING DISEASES.

Saturn being the planet that governs the flesh, it is necessary to consider Saturn first, when diagnosing a case. When Saturn is in a vital sign, more or less inharmony is created there, and much trouble sometimes results. But there is a greater possibility of restoring a person afflicted with consumption when Saturn is in Gemini, the house of the lungs, than when Saturn is in Sagittarius, Pisces or Virgo. The reason for this is because when Saturn is in Gemini he draws other forces to the rescue, but when he is in either of the other three houses, he draws the forces away from the lung section, leaving the activities low and weak. This should always be borne in mind when treating a case of this nature.

This rule applies to all parts of the system, and the following diagrams will illustrate and more fully explain what sections are afflicted by combinations in which Saturn afflicts vital portions of the physical organism.

DIAGRAM 18.

In this horoscope Saturn is in Aries, hence the concentration of all the other vibrations upon that section, and magnet, which has the most vital effect upon the physical health. Mars is in quadrature which indicates inharmonious relations. The Earth is also in quadratic aspect, which makes her sense these conditions very keenly. Libra has no magnet to draw power toward that section, therefore, Libra is being exhausted, taken from, reduced, hence a low and inharmonious vibration must necessarily result, indicating stricture of the intestines, constipation, inflammation of the bowels, and after many attempts to remove the same, kidney and liver difficulties appear, and also sexual weakness, because of the close relation and position to these parts.

THE ONLY CURE.

Proper diet is all that is needed to prevent the above mentioned ailments, and diet alone is the only treatment that will restore harmony to the system of one thus afflicted. See Rules of Diet.

DIAGRAM 18—.

In the case before us, we find Saturn in Taurus, and by applying the same reasoning as in the previous case, we conclude that the sign Scorpio is afflicted, and as Taurus is the section of the nervous system the indications are more serious, from the fact that when the nervous system is weakened, or inharmoniously vibrated, greater danger from diseases must result. We find also in this case that Leo, the heart section has no magnet, therefore that section is weakened by Saturn, which indicates a slow action of the heart. We find Mercury weak in physical vitality which shows more weakness. In arriving at a conclusion in this case, we say first, the sexual organs are greatly afflicted, and the nervous system is in an aggravated condition. So the first thing to do, is to remove, or shut off all food and drink, that in any way irritates or operates upon the nerves. Everything that has a tendency to thicken the blood, must be abandoned, and such diet as is best suited to the case substituted. See Rules of Diet.

TREATMENT.

In cases of rectal disorders, gravel, piles, female weakness, falling of the womb, and various other ailments, all of which are the result of, first, the primal cause or magnetic weakness, and second, the aggravation of the primal affliction

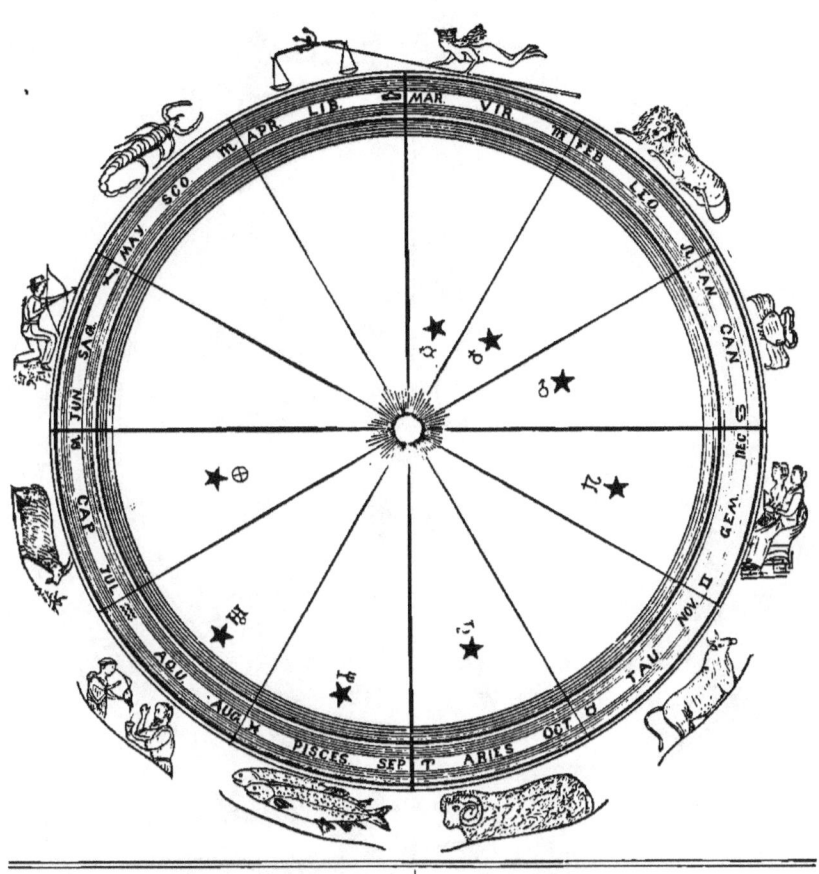

PHYSICAL POWERS.							MENTAL POWERS.					
☿	♀	♂	♃	♄	♅	♆	☿	♀	♂	♃	♄	♅	♆

DIAGRAM No. 18.

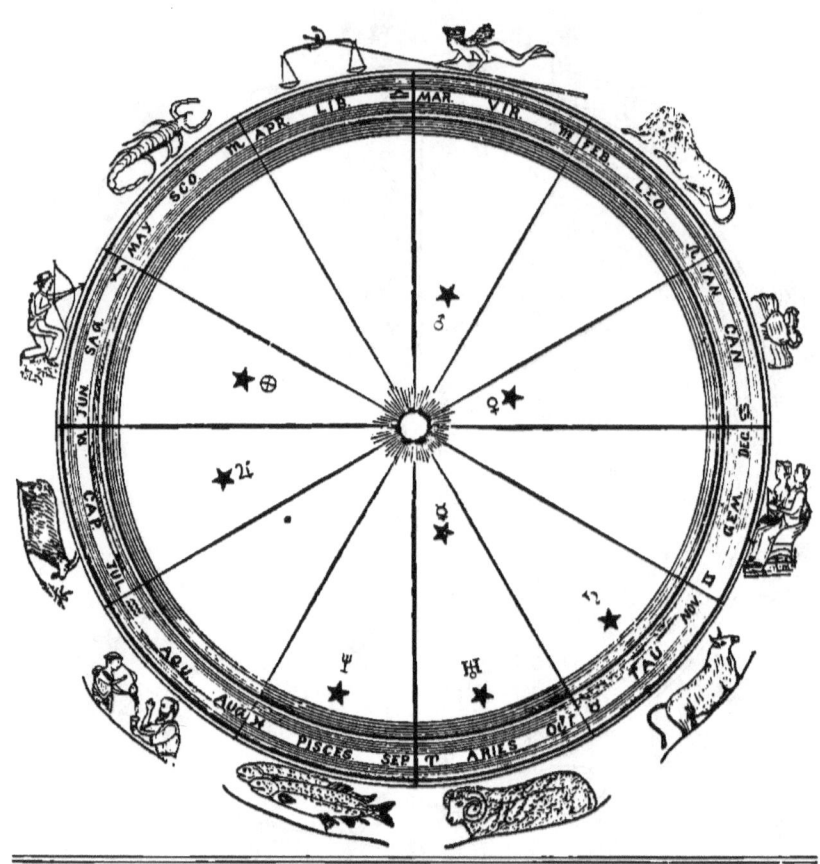

PHYSICAL POWERS.							MENTAL POWERS.						
☿	♀	♂	♃	♄	♅	♆	☿	♀	♂	♃	♄	♅	♆

DIAGRAM No. 18.—

by food, drinks, and drugs, unfit for the system of a Samson. The sitz bath is a very beneficial and harmless remedy, which will draw the fever from the parts, and also increase the circulation of the blood, which is lacking. Plenty of sunlight and outdoor exercise, the sitz bath, and proper use of a family syringe, with pure rain water, in rectal and womb afflictions, will strengthen and restore this section of the physical organism, in ninety-nine cases out of a hundred.

As the sign Leo is afflicted, also in this case, heart trouble is indicated, and many are dropping dead suddenly every day, because of this primal stamp, under planetary law, and because of the polution taken into the system, the impurities of which lodge in the apex of the heart, and suddenly stop the circulation. Proper diet alone will remove all danger from this section.

DIAGRAM 19.

This combination of forces drawn toward the Earth by her conjunction with Saturn in Gemini, indicates considerable trouble with the lungs, but the fact that Saturn is drawing all the other powers in this direction, shows us that these other magnetic effects will give strength and endurance to these parts, and as Venus is in strong aspect to the Earth and Saturn, there is every prospect of recovery in cases of this nature, already started and aggravated. Jupiter being in Aries, indicates mental power which is very important in treating all the ills of the flesh, Mercury also is strong in physical power, giving a full vital life and force to the system. Therefore this case is one that can be cured by the simple method already stated.

DIAGRAM 20.

We now find Saturn in Cancer in conjunction with Venus, the Earth in Virgo in conjunction with Mercury. Mercury indicates high vital powers, Jupiter, Mars, Saturn and Venus aspect the sign Aries, which indicates great mental power. Venus and Jupiter fully balance the effects of Mars and Saturn, and the section of the thighs, or the sign Capricornus, which has no magnet, is but slightly affected, because of this evenness of balance of the forces aspecting that house.

We conclude then, that this combination means health to whoever is born under it, and in case of slight disturbances, and colds, which all are subject to, there is nothing to be feared with persons of this nature.

DIAGRAM 21.

Saturn is alone in Leo in this reading, with Mercury and Uranus, two vitalizers, intensifying the nervous system. The Earth in Cancer, however, is protected somewhat by Venus in quadratic aspect in Aries, but as the first combination is strong upon the heart, the most vital section, there is every indication of a nervous ailment. Palpitation, suffocation, angina pectoris, or neuralgia of the heart, these afflictions are usually named, but the real cause is in the antagonistic magnetic vibrations of that section of the anatomy. Saturn contracts the apex of the heart, while Mercury intensifies the circulation, suddenly, and periodically, when in strong aspect to this sign.

Uranus vibrates the nerve, aura, the mind force, and produces fear, which causes the spirit to abandon the body, that is, give up instead of attempting to control and regain equilibrium.

The treatment of a case of this kind must be such as will calm the nerves, and thin the blood, for the blood is the affected part. It has been rendered thick by food and drink, and food and drink that will thin the same, will remove all danger. See Rules of Diet.

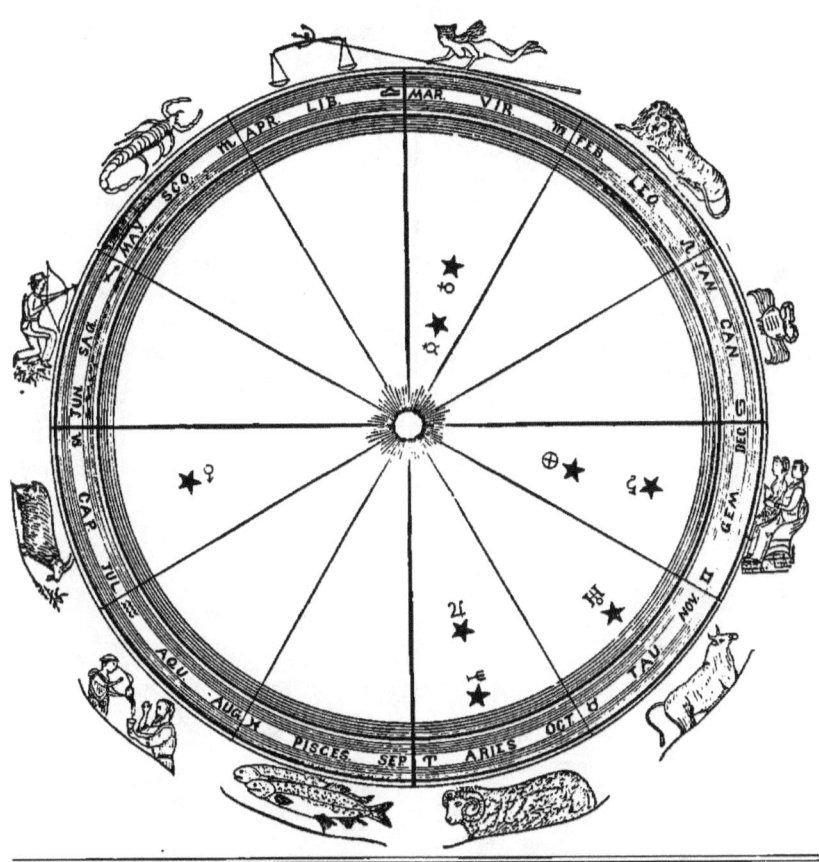

PHYSICAL POWERS.							MENTAL POWERS.						
☿	♀	♂	♃	♄	♅	♆	☿	♀	♂	♃	♄	♅	♆

DIAGRAM No. 19.

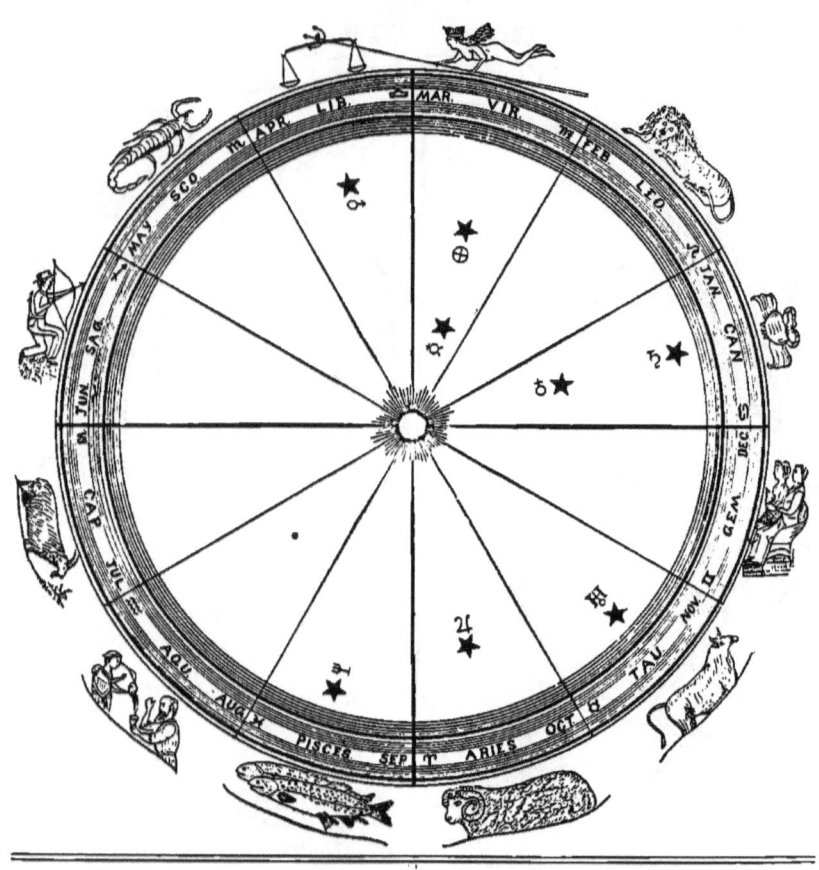

DIAGRAM No. 20.

DIAGRAM 22.

If a person calls or sends for a physical delineation according to this system, and this horoscope of the heavens is found at their birth, we would first consider Saturn in Virgo in triple conjunction with the Earth and Mercury, with Venus and Mars in quadrature in Gemini, and Neptune in opposition. This combination of magnets is very powerful, and signifies a very strong character. Saturn, Neptune, Mars and Mercury, are a bad combination for the lungs, as well as the stomach, and Venus alone is the only counteracting influence. Jupiter, however, protects the heart and nervous system, and Uranus gives mental power and spiritual perception, which makes it possible to keep the spirits up, and active.

We conclude from this lay out that the stomach is more intensely operated upon than any other portion of the system. As Mercury, the quickener, is in that sign, the magnetic forces are antagonistic, hence the derangement of the same, and kidney and liver complaints will be the result, but no serious cases need be anticipated, except when the conditions are greatly aggravated.

A simple treatment is all that is necessery to restore harmony. On account of the inharmonious vibrations centering upon the stomach, the food is not fomented harmoniously, hence does not assimilate freely. A coating is liable to form on account of this, and to remove this and cleanse the stomach, is the first thing to do. Vinegar contains enough acetic acid to cut out this coating and acidify and purify the same, therefore a diet consisting of potatoes, cabbage, onions sliced in vinegar, pickles and cider, are necessary to pacify the stomach, vivify the liver and kidneys and create a more even and harmonious assimilation and circulation. One such meal a day, with nuts, fruits and cereals, as given in Rules of Diet, will

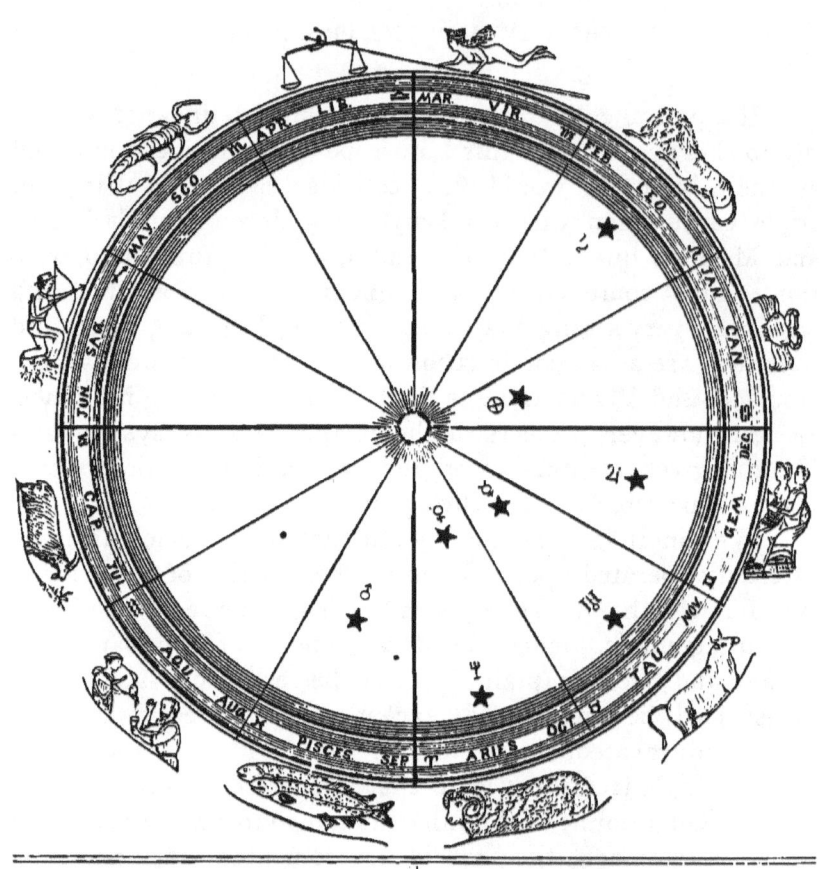

DIAGRAM No. 21.

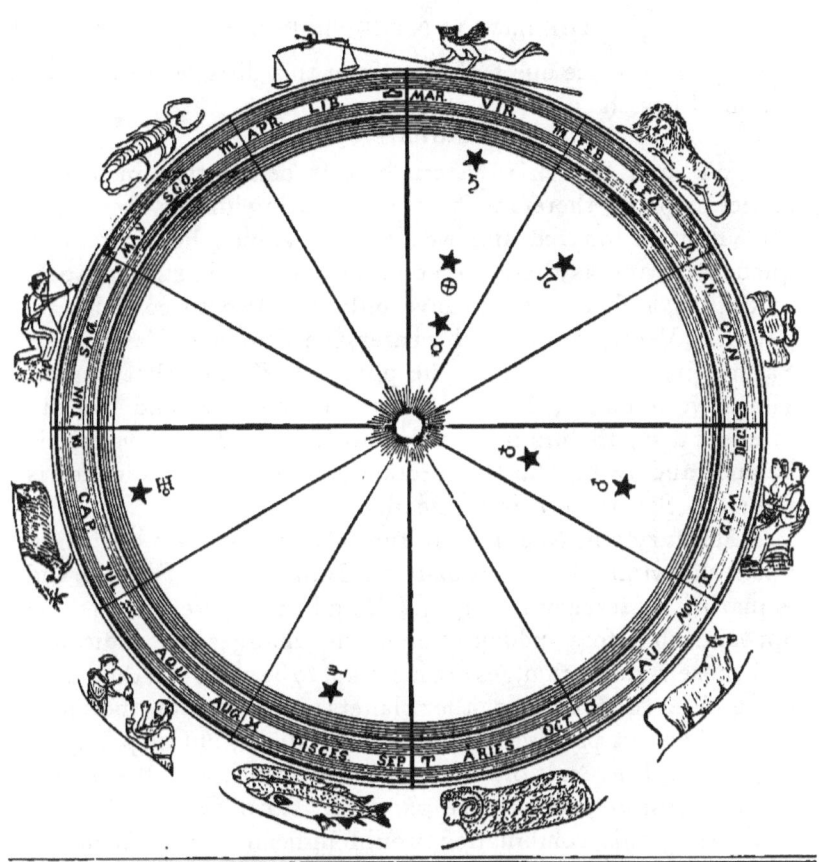

PHYSICAL POWERS.							MENTAL POWERS.						
☿	♀	♂	♃	♄	♅	♆	☿	♀	♂	♃	♄	♅	♆

DIAGRAM No. 22.

very quickly place one suffering from this disorder into a condition of health.

DIAGRAM 23.

We find Saturn in Libra in this delineation, in strong aspect to Aries, therefore the brain is being drawn from, and the vibration lowered and weakened. Venus, however, is in quadrature and as there are no other magnets in strong aspect to Saturn and Venus we have only the two to consider together. Venus being much nearer the Sun and Earth than Saturn, just about balances the physical effect of that planet. Hence we conclude, that as Venus is harmonious and healthy in effect upon the brain, that the two will produce a very fair balance and average in that section, so no serious indication is found by Saturn in this delineation.

Mercury and Neptune are the only two magnets operating upon the vital physical quadrate, Taurus, Leo, Scorpio and Aquarius. Mercury is very quick and active, Neptune is the opposite, therefore sudden strains and changes are indicated, and these sudden changes are more apt to be paralytic than anything else. If these and other planets are near or on the meridians, there is positive evidence of paralysis, but as paralysis is generally the result of constipation, proper food will prevent, and also restore such a case as this. With Saturn changed to Scorpio, this combination would indicate paralysis of the heart, also locomotor ataxia, and with Venus giving a strong desire for things palatable, the case would be one requiring skill in treating the mind of the patient, as well as the body.

DIAGRAM 24.

The horoscope for this lesson, shows the positions of the planets on the third day of February, 1895. Saturn is in conjunction with Uranus in the sign Scorpio, a vital sign. Mercury is in opposition in Taurus, the section of the nervous system. The three are in quadrature to the sign Leo, in which the Earth is moving. All of the other magnets are weak, both upon the Earth, and upon Saturn, Mercury and Uranus. Therefore, this is a very powerful combination of inharmonious vibrations, polarized to the nervous system, and especially to the heart. All persons still in the dark concerning the law of physical life and health, will suffer, and many will succumb under this pressure, the heart will simply stop and they will be forced to vacate at once. Persons magnetically related, and we mean by this, those who were afflicted in the heart section by Saturn's aspect at the time of their birth, who are drinking coffee freely, which has a tendency to thicken the blood and aggravate the nervous system, will suffer the most. The blood being thick and the heart section being contracted by Saturn, and inharmoniously vibrated by Uranus, when Mercury comes swiftly, and suddenly into Taurus, and starts the blood and heart instantly into rapid action, the result is an explosion, and death relieves the soul from bondage.

TREATMENT.

Many people will not feel that there is any danger in their heart difficulties, therefore, they will do nothing to prevent this culmination. Of course they will know nothing about the magnetic law, and will not be prepared to meet it. But to those who are afflicted with heart troubles of any kind, a warning and suggestion should be sufficient. As already stated, the blood is thickened by Saturn, as well as by coffee, and indigestible food. The only thing necessary to do, in order to remove all danger, is to thin up the blood and cleanse the system. Then when Mercury springs into the sign Taurus, the same activity of the heart and blood will be produced, but the blood will be in a condition to flow freely, and

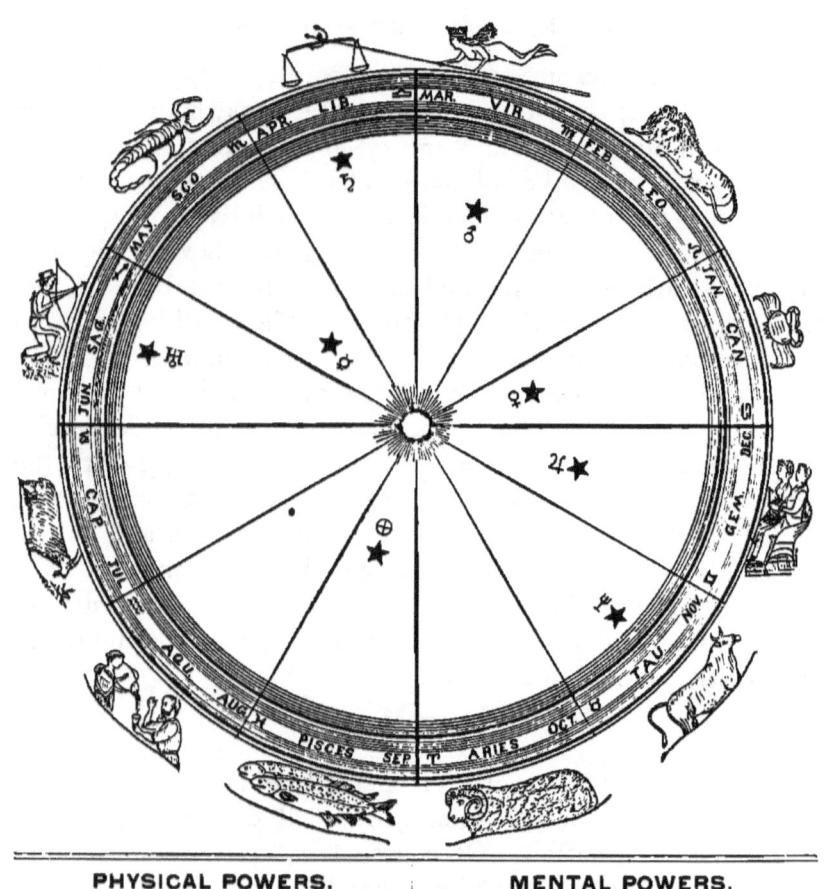

DIAGRAM No. 23

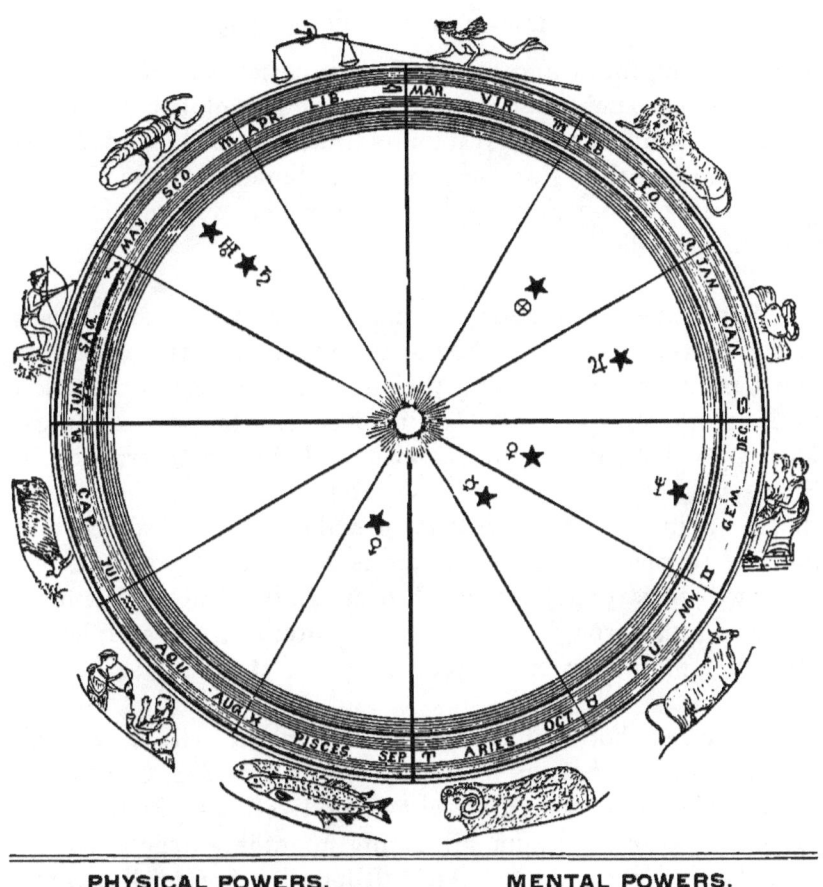

PHYSICAL POWERS.							MENTAL POWERS.						
☿	♀	♂	♃	♄	♅	♆	☿	♀	♂	♃	♄	♅	♆

DIAGRAM No. 24.

only a slight shock and pain will be experienced. Other difficulties of a sexual nature will appear, and trouble both sexes, but the treatment of the system as indicated, will restore harmony and health. For there is no combination of the planets, the bad effects of which cannot be controlled, and reduced to a very slight affliction.

DIAGRAM 25.

September 17th, 1897, the planets will be in the houses or signs indicated by the horoscope for this lesson. Saturn and Uranus will be entering the sign Sagittarius in opposition to Neptune in the sign Gemini, the section of the lungs. Mercury will be in Sagittarius also, and the Earth will be in Pisces, in quadrature to the combination. This means to those having lung difficulties, a sudden tearing down and racking to pieces, but as Jupiter is high in physical power, there will be strength imparted to the Earth which will enable many to pull through, until Jupiter enters Libra and leaves the bad combination to complete its work the next season, or year.

Children born under this combination will have the strengthening influence of Jupiter on the stomach, and lungs, therefore will be comparatively long lived, as Jupiter, Neptune, Mars and Uranus, all acting together, denote power, tenacity and continuity. And although more or less lung affections are indicated, unless such characters are very careless and negligent, they will not have consumption. Those who are afflicted by other combinations, indicating consumption, will at this time suffer very much, and many will pass away during Mercury's stay in conjunction with Saturn.

DIAGRAM 26.

In the foregoing diagram, we find Saturn in Capricornus, in quadrature to the Earth and Uranus in Aries. The other planets are weak in aspect to these three. The Earth is in the sign of fevers, the sign of the head. Uranus is drawing the forces of Saturn and the other planets toward that sign, while Saturn is pulling toward Capricornus. All of which weakens the two sections, Libra and Cancer. Mercury is weak, hence the vitality is very low. Saturn and Uranus are inharmonious, therefore, friction and exhaustion must result. Cancer and Libra being afflicted indicate bowel difficulty, and low activity in the chest. The bowel contraction means a constipated condition.

This in turn means feverish afflictions, and general polution of the system from lack of circulation. The bowels are a section that can be operated upon, hence the removal of the obstruction in that section. The section of the chest is not supposed to be treated for anything unless there is something there to treat, so this section is overlooked in a case of this kind, and the bowels receive most of the medicine, food and attention. All the time there is gathering in this cess pool of low vibrating atoms, and contracted arteries and veins, the impurities of the blood, the thickened and clotted particles that cannot pass these contracted parts. This is so silent and so gradual that it is not noticed until a hard lump is formed and pressed toward the surface. An examination discloses the fact that it is a case of cancer of the breast. Fear and consternation takes possession of the mind at once, and the cancer fiend, and exterminator is consulted. He, or she, for they are too numerous to mention, both male and female, and not one of them have any idea of the cause of such manifestations, makes a great scare by telling of the wonderful cases they have treated. One uses plasters, another the knife, and some use internal remedies, while others use mind force, electricity, magnetism, and various other forces and systems. Nearly all

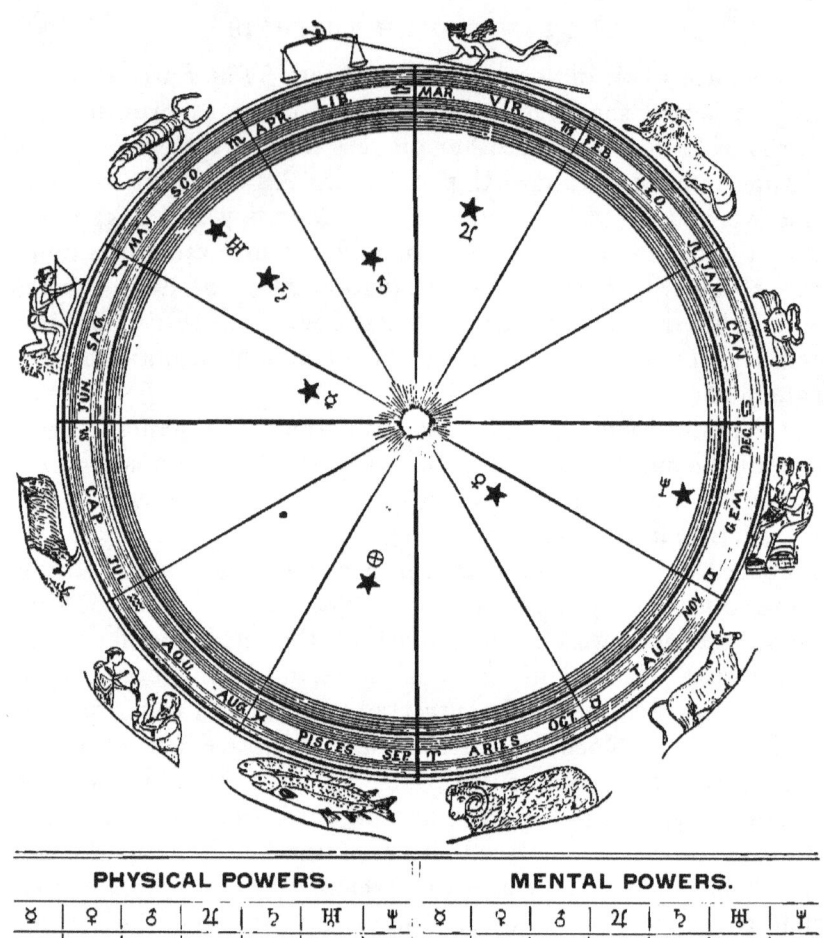

PHYSICAL POWERS.								MENTAL POWERS.						
☿	♀	♂	♃	♄	♅	♆		☿	♀	♂	♃	♄	♅	♆

DIAGRAM No. 25.

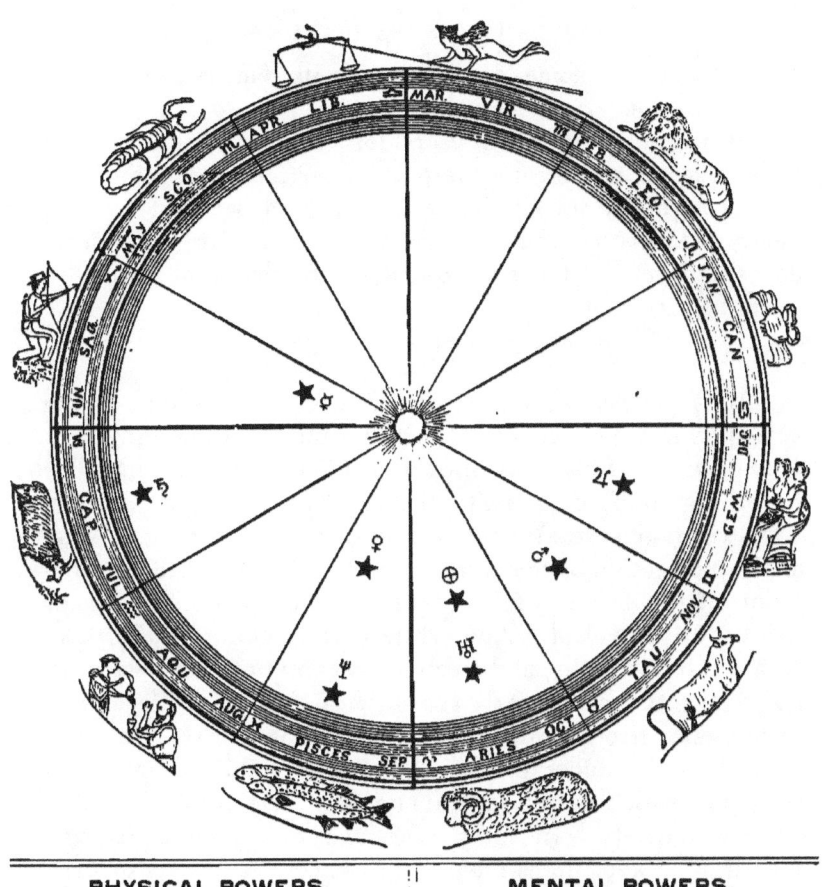

DIAGRAM No. 26.

of them have the same idea concerning its removal, which is to get it out at once. Remove it.

It has probably taken years for these small particles of blood to settle and form a lump. The arteries and veins leading through this section being clogged, warped and twisted, finally present the appearance of an animal with many legs, horns, tails, etc. Hence the one desire to have it out whole so it can be seen.

TREATMENT OF CANCER.

It is useless to attempt to remove a cancer as long as the system is in a condition to feed it, by continuing to lodge impure particles of blood within this section of the system. The first thing to be done is to thoroughly cleanse the system. This will take several months in most cases, but just as soon as the circulation of the bowels is restored, and a healthy condition of the same is fully realized, the growth of the cancer will be fully checked. And while this is going on, Turkish baths, sulphur baths, and frequent sweating of the chest, with hot, wet cloths, will greatly assist in passing off the fever and in restoring circulation, and strength to the chest. Plenty of sunlight and outdoor exercise should be indulged in, all of this time, which means several months. The cancer should be ignored entirely. In most cases if this diet, exercise and breathing is kept up as long as it has taken the cancer to form, there will be nothing more to do, for it will disappear as silently and surely as it came. If, however, after several months of preparation, and gaining of strength, and vivifying the section afflicted by physical exercise, breathing exercises, etc., it is deemed expedient to assist nature in the removal, a surgeon may be called who should lance the cancer, open it up slightly, and then it should be poulticed with slippery elm, flax seed or some softening and harmless application, which will gradually draw it to a head, and remove the same without danger. This should be done very slowly, a month is a short time to bring such a lump to a head. To prevent children growing up, and yet to be born from having such difficulties, feed them as they should be fed, and teach them how to vibrate their physical organisms by breathing exercises. See lesson on breathing.

DIAGRAM 27.

We find the heavenly magnets scattered very evenly around the Sun, in the horoscope before us. Saturn in Aquarius would, under some combinations, mean heart trouble, and a generally nervous condition. But as Venus and Jupiter are both in Leo, in strong aspect to the sign Taurus, this bad indication of Saturn's position is rendered harmless, and with so much that is good from Venus and Jupiter, the general health is indicated as very good.

We find a combination strong upon the Earth, however, that is not so pleasant. Neptune is in Aries, in quadrature to the Earth and Mercury, and in opposition to Mars. Neptune signifies coldness, dampness, and stiffness in the limbs. Mercury indicates fevers, by aspect to Aries. Mars also intensifies the effect of Mercury. Therefore chills and fevers are indicated very clearly. A fever of some kind must, necessarily, culminate the life of a person born under these influences.

The antidote for conditions of this kind are the things themselves; that is to say, when Neptune is strong in aspect, cold drinks, and water is best of all, should be freely used, outwardly and inwardly. When Mercury, or Mars, comes into effect, hot drinks and food is best. Systems of this nature require sours extensively in their daily diet.

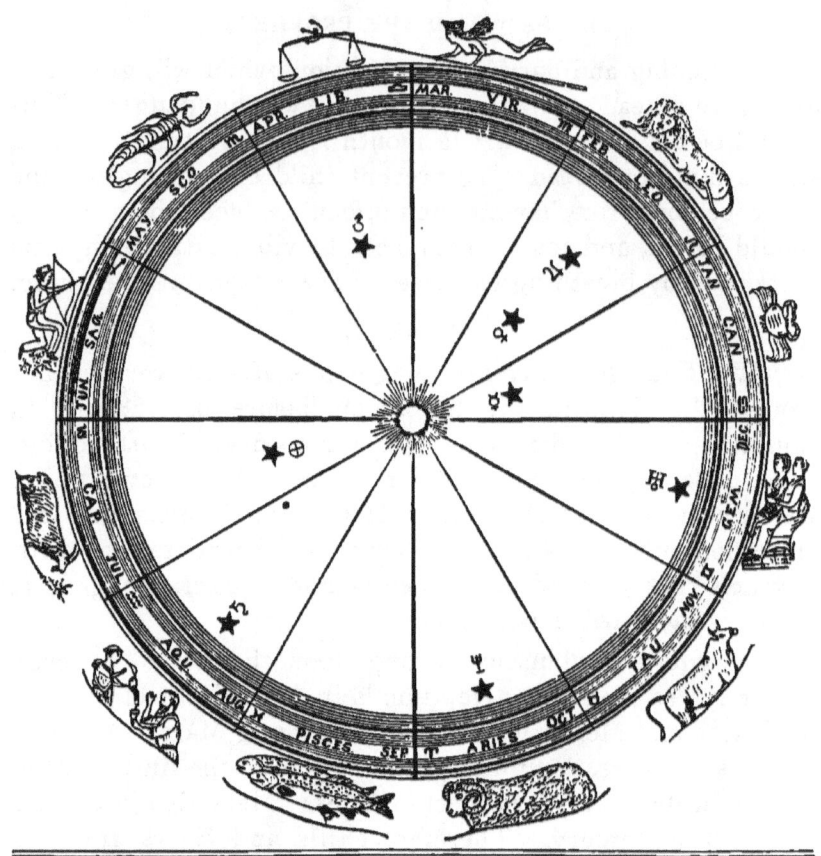

DIAGRAM No. 27.

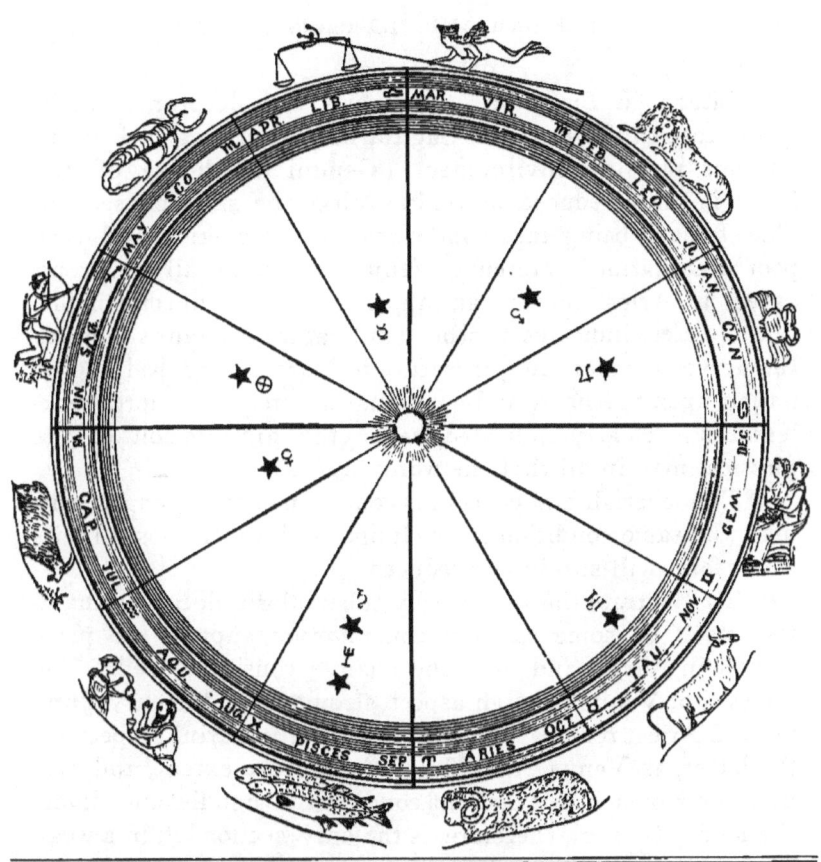

PHYSICAL POWERS.							MENTAL POWERS.						
☿	♀	♂	♃	♄	♅	♆	☿	♀	♂	♃	♄	♅	♆

DIAGRAM No. 28.

DIAGRAM 28.

Saturn in Pisces in conjunction with Neptune and in quadrature to the Earth in Sagittarius, indicates a bad condition for physical environment. Gemini the house of the lungs is being reduced, as well as Virgo the stomach section. The stomach being tardy indicates weak digestion and very poor assimilation. Mercury, Venus and Jupiter all in strong aspect to Aries, reveals an appetite that is uncontrolable. Mars in Leo, indicates a rather hard nature. Uranus vibrates the nervous system in quadrature to Mars, a very bad combination upon the heart and emotional nature. In short, recklessness is clearly indicated, hence, the gratification of the physical man in all that the word implies.

The feverish and cancerous condition of the stomach, will meet the same condition in the lungs, and tuberculosis in its worst form will surely be produced.

To illustrate the reason why tuberculosis does not manifest itself in some cases of consumption, suppose we place Venus in Virgo, and note the change thus produced. The removal of Venus from an aspect strong with Mercury, Jupiter and Aries, removes the desire for food and drink, especially the latter, as Venus rules fluids, to a great extent, and also puts the stomach in excellent condition to handle and digest the food. Gemini, therefore, is the only section left in a weak condition, a case of this nature would not be nearly so severe, but Venus is yielding in nature, and as Mercury indicates low vitality and feverish tendencies, the affliction is consumption just the same. This last case would be curable, while the former would not be, generally speaking. The assimilation of the food in this latter case would prevent tuberculosis in most cases, and a slower, lingering, trial would be the result, if improperly treated.

Why is it necessary to make farther explanations concerning the treatment of diseases, after having repeatedly stated that pollution alone is what aggravates and intensifies the primal weakness. Food alone will prevent disease, and food alone will permanently cure the same. Nature will always restore natural conditions if given an opportunity to do her work. The healing balm in the air of the natural forest is very beneficial, and probably one of the greatest healing agencies given by nature for this disease, is balsam, and the patient should gather it in the forest and eat it on the spot, together with natural fruits, nuts, etc.

The phlegmatic condition must be cut out and the parts healed. This balsam is the best thing known to thus revolutionize these conditions, and restore strength and harmony. It is not a good plan to change climates, but far better to get out and use the climate adapted to. The nearest wood where spruce, hemlock, balsam and pine are found is the place for those who are yet able to get around. Those who are not can be surrounded with these natural odors, and the balsam blisters can be brought in fresh, by stripping the tree of its bark. Limbs of hemlock, pine, spruce, cedar, and tamarack should surround every patient suffering with consumption, and with proper food most cases are curable.

Following these twenty-four delineations are three horoscopes of the heavenly magnets, corresponding to the respective dates of three of the world's most famous, orators, statesmen, and travelers: Abraham Lincoln, Robert G. Ingersoll, and George Francis Train. As these characters are well known there is nothing new to be said about them, but certain

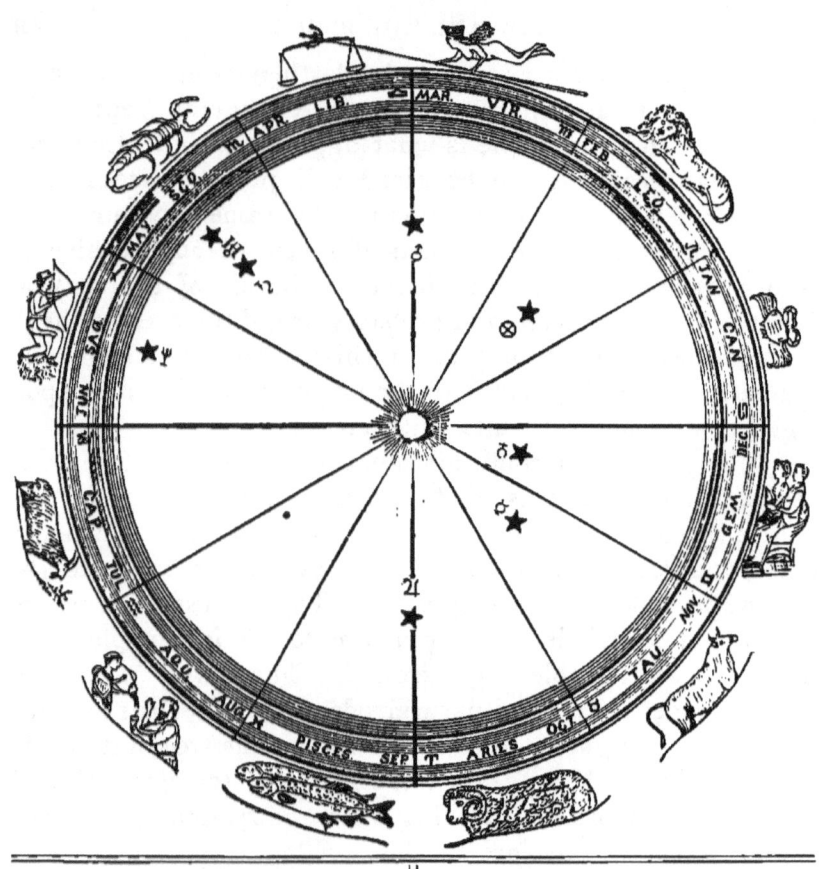

PHYSICAL POWERS.							MENTAL POWERS.						
☿	♀	♂	♃	♄	♅	♆	☽	♀	♂	♃	♄	♅	♆
93	84	45	81	51	66	36	80	68	53	62	44	44	17

DIAGRAM No. 29.

magnetic reasons for their greatness will be interesting in connection with this work. Therefore the magnetic law of their dates is given.

DIAGRAM 29.

ABRAHAM LINCOLN.

The above calculation shows us the magnetic forces of the planets when Abraham Lincoln was stamped as an individual magnet, destined to become the head of this great nation. We find Mercury was the ruling magnet both physical and mental at a very high pressure. Venus ruled high also, and Jupiter run high in physical power, and being on the line of Aries and Pisces he was in a powerful position to draw all forces to him. Hence the mental power to lead and control, so ably manifested by this noble character. Mars in opposition, indicated leadership also, being on the line between Virgo and Libra. Mercury, Saturn and Uranus quadrating the Earth, and Leo, the heart sign, also indicates a nerve that is hard to battle with, and a dangerous character to cope with in battle or in anything else. Venus in opposition to Neptune also strong upon the Earth, shows friendly relations with distant nations and people. The Earth being in Leo indicates a very emotional nature, and Uranus in quadrature, signifies spirituality, but the heart is afflicted by Saturn, Uranus and Mercury, hence a very nervous and excitable, and irritable constitution. The planets are evenly balanced about the Sun and they are all in strong aspects to each other. Therefore a strong character is indicated. The two red war gods, Mars and Jupiter, both being on meridians, indicate leadership, and Mercury, Saturn and Uranus indicate heart affliction. Therefore, sudden death was natural to this character. Heart disease would probably have terminated the life had he been spared longer.

Mr. Lincoln was not an orator, or very much of a speech maker, he lacked that verbal expression so characteristic of Mr. Ingersoll. Geo. Francis Train, even has more logical utterances than Mr. Lincoln, yet he has much less fluency than the Colonel. Jupiter being on the line between the positive pole, or sign Aries, which represents the head, and Pisces the negative pole of the feet, may, or may not have had something to do with the length of Mr. Lincoln's framework. The fact remains, however, that Jupiter is a powerful magnet and is in most potent position for leadership that is possible for him to be.

DIAGRAM 30.

GEO. FRANCIS TRAIN.

[Mr. Train kindly gave me the date of his birth at the Palmer House, Chicago, on the occasion of a private meeting with a number of Magi Mystics, when four hours passed as a minute, so interesting was the conversation.]

We find the Earth has just entered Libra, and as Libra is in strong aspect to Aries, the perception is very keen, concerning physical things. Libra being the physical sign. Saturn and Neptune are exactly opposite each other and in quadrature to the Earth, and the sign Aries. Therefore, Saturn and Neptune evenly balance the mind. It will be noticed in this horoscope, the same as in Mr. Lincoln's, that the planets are all in powerful aspect to each other. None weak, and alone. This always indicates strong forceful characters. Saturn has been in Libra for two years, 1892 and 1893. When Saturn crossed the line leading into Libra, Mr. Train opened his mouth with speech. He had been silent for several years.

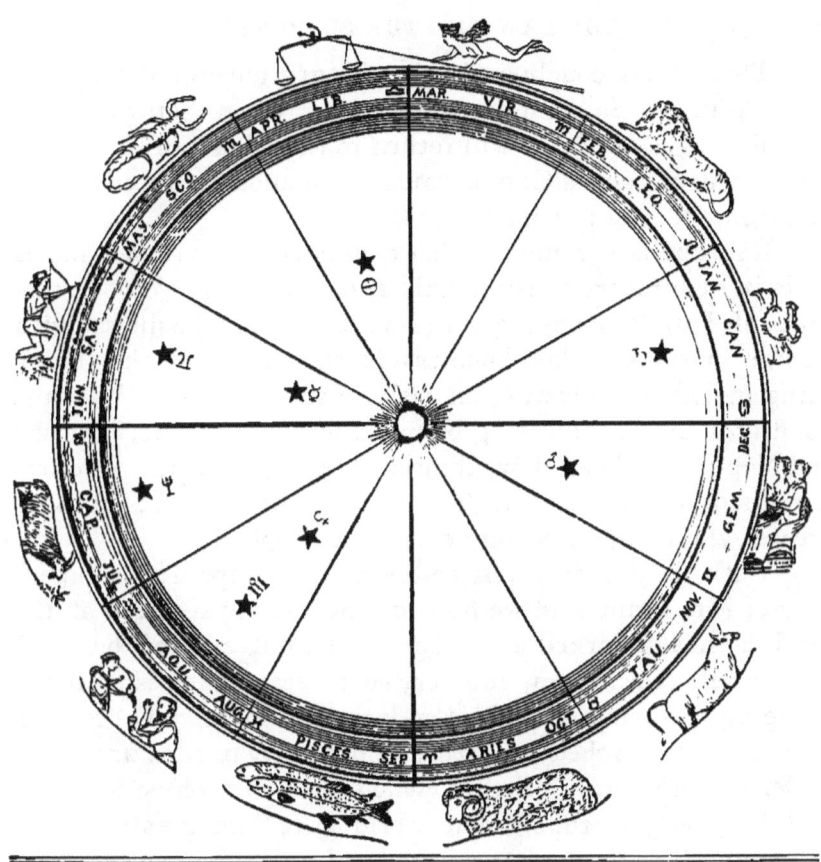

DIAGRAM No. 30.

This proves conclusively that Saturn governs the speech of Mr. Train. So we must expect that when Saturn enters Scorpio, that Mr. Train will return to the silence, and remain until Saturn reaches Capricornus, when another impulse will be given, for him to speak.

Neptune is the magnet that causes people to travel, and as he is in quadrature to the Earth and Aries, it is very significant of long journeyings, sea voyages, and business with foreign nations. The business is the result of the Earth being in Libra, indicating an early business career. Neptune quadrates Libra, indicating business under Neptune. Saturn and Neptune indicate low vibrations throughout the physical organism, therefore, Mr. Train does not feel the chilling breezes and damp atmosphere as most people do.

With these indications before us, we compare the experience of Mr. Train, and we find that he has always been at the head, he never worked a day for others, but entered business for himself at nineteen, and very soon became interested in the shipping industry, and done a large business with foreign nations. He reached his greatest popularity in 1892 and 1893, under the influence of Saturn which came into physical glory, in Libra, early in 1892. The world gave him greater recognition and became more interested in his prophetic utterances.

Owing to Uranus and Venus being in weak position and aspect, Mr. Train brings everything to the material plane, and treats it purely from that standpoint, yet Saturn gives him the vision of prophecy.

DIAGRAM 31.
ROBERT G. INGERSOLL.

We have before us a most wonderful combination of magnetic forces. Observe that all the planets are in conjunction. The Earth is in Aquarius, in conjunction with Uranus. This

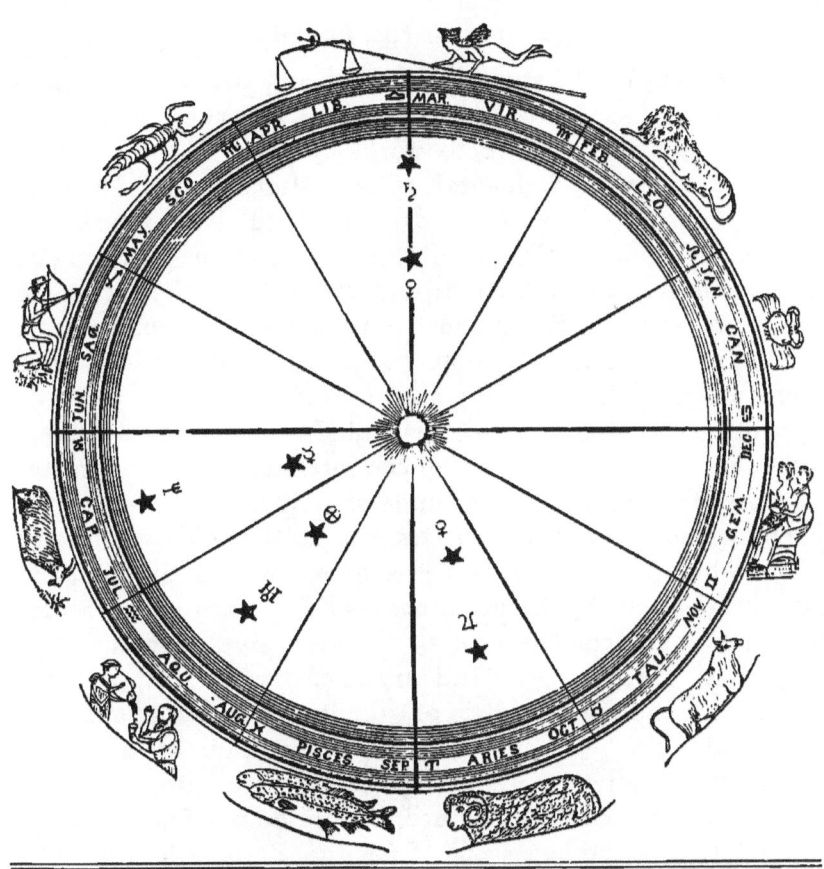

PHYSICAL POWERS.							MENTAL POWERS.						
☿	♀	♂	♃	♄	♅	♆	☿	♀	♂	♃	♄	♅	♆
47	74	41	86	47	56	41	74	80	59	68	47	35	38

DIAGRAM No. 31.

signifies a spiritual nature. Uranus being the spiritual magnet as already explained. It also means a worker, with nerve force, energy, and a desire to work. Jupiter is the physical ruler, while Venus is mental ruler. Mercury and Neptune are in quadrature to Venus and Jupiter, and also to Mars and Saturn, in Libra. Think of this combination of magnetic forces polarized in such strong aspects to Aries, the section of the brain, with the Earth and Uranus aspecting Leo, the heart and emotional section. Jupiter balances Saturn, and Venus evens up with Mars, making a brain force that is capable of hypnotising an army of ordinary minds. Mercury and Neptune only quicken and broaden the intellect and give greater capacity for research and understanding. Mercury gives fluent speech by aspect to Aries, the section of speech, also wit and humor. Venus in Aries gives that soft, tender, and sympathetic tone to the utterances, while Mars gives accuracy, precision and combativeness. Jupiter gives oratory and eloquence, Saturn, logic and argument, while Neptune encircles the whole with a halo of grandeur, that captivates the mind and soul. We find in the combination of Mercury, Venus and Jupiter, the same indication corcerning appetite, drink, etc., previously explained, and we do not find any such combination in the horoscope of George Francis Train. Observe what these two positions or horoscopes signify. In Mr. Ingersoll's case, the appetite is very keen, and the desire to gratify the appetite will be very intense. But the danger of so doing is greatly lessened by the other magnets operating upon the brain, giving a powerful intellect and character. Nevertheless the Colonel will have to use more or less will force to keep the appetite within bounds.

In the case of Mr. Train, there never was a very keen appetite. Therefore he has long since given up the use of flesh food, and stimulating beverages, and feels that he has won a victory over the appetite. The greatest victory is won by the person who has the appetite to begin with, and then overcomes and puts away these things, as many have done.

We might search out the living exemplifications of this wonderful magnetic law of physical environment for a century, and in every instance we would find that greatness is the result of a favorable horoscope, while the opposite is found in those who are unfavorably blessed with magnetic forces at birth.

There is a quality in soul, in astral development, which can only be considered *by the soul*, or inner consciousness, which determines greatness in human life, and which is the impelling power in each human organism. It is interesting to select from the multitudes we meet, those souls who in the past were bred and born, reared, trained and purified in those mystical schools of attainment, which flourished in Greece and Rome, and produced the wonderful physical beauty, and intellectual genius, the records of which stand to-day as a monument to their superiority and power. Those who are able to see beyond the veil of flesh, recognize those souls who passed the crucial test of those times.

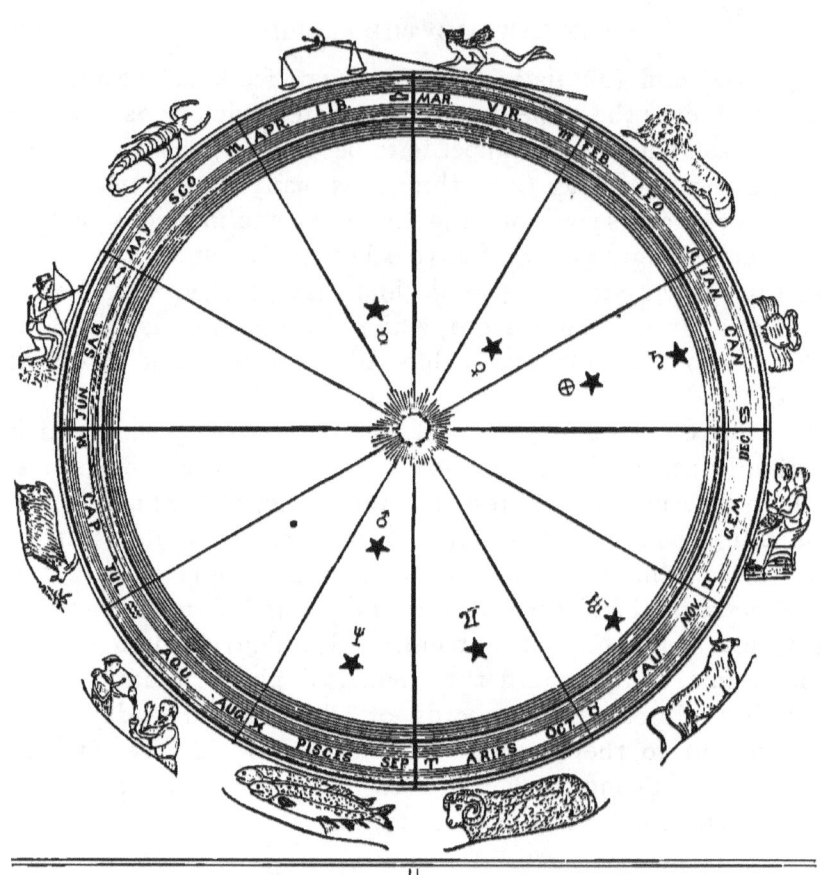

PHYSICAL POWERS.							MENTAL POWERS.					
☿	♀	♂	♃	♄	♅	♆	☿	♀	♂	♃	♄	♅	♆
67	88	76	94	88	58	46	88	64	37	75	73	49	13

DIAGRAM No. 32.

DIAGRAM 32.
QUESTIONS AND ANSWERS.

QUESTION.—Where is the Earth in the above horoscope?
ANSWER.—In the house or sign of Cancer.

Q.—In what quarter of the heavens is the sign Cancer located?

A.—In the second quarter.

Q.—Why is it called the second quarter?

A.—Because as we begin to count the degrees of the celestial Zodiac with the first degree of Aries, we complete one quarter of the circle when we reach Cancer. Hence, the first degree of Cancer is the beginning of the second quarter. Therefore, we say the Earth is in the second quarter, the quarter of wisdom, when in Cancer.

Q.—What do we mean by the quarter of wisdom? Why is it called the quarter of wisdom?

A.—Because while the Earth is passing through this quarter, it is the season of winter, the season of intellectual pursuits, the season for contemplation, for mental activity, for intelligent reasoning, and spiritual attainment.

Q.—Why is this more possible in this quarter than in any other quarter?

A.—Because during the other three quarters of the year, the physical man is more expressive, and active. Hence there is less concentration and research into the deeper and more secret realm, where intelligence dwells.

Q.—What significance does this quarter convey in delineating a character born here?

A.—It signifies that they are naturally intelligent, and are capable of attainment in intellectual pursuits, and that they tend in that direction naturally.

Q.—What is the significance of the sign Cancer in the above figure?

A.—It shows by quadratic aspect to the sign Aries, that a person born at the time will be very active mentally, quick, bright, and clear of perception, and capable of giving utterance to the thought and feelings, in clear and expressive language.

Q.—What other conditions, or influences do we find in connection with the sign Cancer?

A.—We find the planet Saturn is in Cancer, in conjunction or seventh aspect to the Earth, at 88% of physical, and 73% of mental power.

Q.—What is the significance of Saturn in this horoscope?

A.—Saturn being in perihelion, and in conjunction with the Earth, which is also in perihelion, causes very strong magnetic relations, the physical effect of which is very intense. This aspect of Saturn, therefore, signifies a character somewhat inharmonious and discontented; a character that continually yearns for something, and is never quite satisfied with anything. But as Saturn is in quadrature to the sign Aries, and the Earth is the same in aspect, Saturn signifies a yearning for knowledge, for spiritual enlightenment; a tenacious and determined mind and will; one which will debate, argue, and question.

Q.—What other physical influence is indicated by Saturn?

A.—Saturn being in strong aspect to Aries, the head, will cause feverish, and nervous conditions; and being also in quadrature to Libra, the bowels are afflicted, and a constipated condition will be the result.

Q.—As Saturn is in Cancer, in such strong magnetic relation to the Earth, does it not indicate cancerous afflictions?

A.—No. Because Saturn is a large magnet, hence is drawing the forces from all the other planets towards him, and their combined forces make a strong constitution, when Saturn is in vital signs, or the mental signs.

Q.—Which is the ruling planet in this horoscope?

A.—Jupiter is the physical ruler, and Mercury is the mental ruler.

Q.—Why is Jupiter the physical ruler?

A.—Because the power of Jupiter is higher than that of any other planet in its physical relation to the Earth.

Q.—As Jupiter is in Aries, the sign of the head, why is he not the mental ruler, also?

A.—Because Jupiter does not produce so marked an effect upon the mental activities, as does the planet Mercury, and as Mercury is in opposition aspect to the sign Aries, Mercury is the mental ruler because highest in mental effect.

Q.—What is the significance of Jupiter in this reading?

A.—Jupiter being in Aries, the sign of the head and brains, produces a strong mind, a powerful brain, and a healthy and harmonious mental nature; great capacity for mental labors is the chief result of Jupiter's position and aspect.

Q.—What is the effect of the planet Jupiter in connection with the planet Saturn in this combination?

A.—Jupiter gives mental power, harmony, and evenness of expression. Saturn is a disturbing force, but very powerful and tenacious in nature. The two show great force of mind and character, and they combine and make a condition that qualifies people from the beginning to take the lead in affairs of the world, especially the intellectual world.

Q.—What planet comes next in physical power, and what does it portend?

A.—Venus is the second planet in physical effect, and rules in this combination at 88%, in her perihelion house Leo. She is in third position or juxtaposition to the Earth, therefore she is weak in aspect. But being in Leo, the house of the heart, and in quadrature to the sign Taurus, which includes the nervous system, the physical effect of Venus is very important in this calculation, for the nervous system, the circulation of the blood, and the physical body generally is made harmonious and healthy. The mental effect is low, hence the expressions of persons born under these percentages of magnetic forces, will be somewhat blunt and harsh, as Venus is out of aspect to Aries. The affections will be general, and universal, and never centered very intensely upon one person. This is because Venus is weak in aspect to the Earth.

Q.—We find Mars weak in aspect, being in third position or bi-quadrature, yet high in percentage of power. Why is this?

A.—Because Mars rules the alimentary canals leading to the stomach, and also the windpipe which leads to the lungs, and as Mars is in the perihelion section of his orbit in very strong aspect to Virgo, the stomach section, and Gemini the lung section, the physical effect is high. The mental effect however, of Mars is very weak owing to the weak aspect to Aries. Therefore, the combative characteristic produced by Mars, is very weak. The mental quality of Mars, which includes mathematics, system, and accuracy, will be lacking in persons born on this date.

Q.—What is the significance of Mercury in the calculation?

A.—The physical effect of Mercury is feverish in nature,

on account of being in strong aspect to Aries, the sign of fire, and being in quadrature to Saturn will conflict more or less with that planet in circulating the blood. But Jupiter will offset Saturn and the result will be generally a good balance. Mercury, therefore, will cause hot flashes, and light fevers, of short duration. The skin will be somewhat tough as a result. The mental effect is very marked, as Mercury is the mental ruler. This indicates a quick, active brain, clear perception, and highly developed intuition. Also fluent speech, and ready wit. The influence of Mercury makes this one of the best combinations for mental achievement that could be desired.

Q.—How does the planet Uranus influence this combination?

A.—Uranus is the planet of nerve force, energy, labor, science, religion, and spirituality, and is in the house of Taurus, the section of the nervous and muscular system. The physical effect of which is to cause a person born on this date to work energetically and continually. The mental percentage being weak, this magnet does not effect the spiritual nature to any great extent, in this calculation. Venus being in Leo, in quadrature, harmonizes the rigid tendencies of Uranus, making a favorable combination of magnetic vibrations for a good physical balance.

Q.—Delineate the planet Neptune in connection with this date and aspect.

A.—Neptune is the planet that gives people the desire to travel, to reach out, to change, and enlarge the possessions, both material and mental. But being weak in aspect to the Earth, the effect is slight. Hence, these characters will not care to travel, except to carry on their labors, and intellectual pursuits. As Neptune is in quadratic aspect to the lung section, persons born at this time will be subject to chills in the back and shoulders, and will take cold easily.

Q.—What bearing does the Moon, which is nearing the last quarter, have upon persons born at this time?

A.—The Moon simply indicates the polarization of the physical expression. That is to say, in expressing the feelings and emotions, these characters need to cultivate the mind, the will, in order to hold the physical feelings and emotions where they belong, when giving utterance to their views.

Q.—Why is this so?

A.—Because the Moon is polarized in a section below the solar plexus, and has a tendency to draw the mind, the thought, the positive principle, the force and energy, toward its polar center, requiring a higher soul force and intellectual power to change, convert, or connect this principle with the forces produced by the other magnets in their relation to the sign Aries, the section of expression, speech, intelligence and positiveness.

Q.—What would be the effect if the Moon was in its new phase?

A.—As the planets, Earth, Saturn, Mercury and Jupiter, are polarized to the positive sign Aries, if the Moon was also in its new phase, it too would be polarized to the same point, hence a most positive condition for mental expression would be the result.

Q.—After considering all of the forces and aspects in this horoscope, what is the most important indication of disease?

A.—As Mercury and Saturn are the principal magnets which must be figured on in physical disturbances, we find that Saturn is in strong aspect to the sign Libra, which includes the bowels, and indicates slow action, and in consequence a feverish condition, which is greatly intensified by

Mercury. Therefore, the conclusion is that constipation will result, and will be the primal cause of physical disturbances. As Jupiter is also in strong aspect to Libra, the bad effect of Mercury and Saturn is greatly lessened, so the bowel difficulty will not be serious. But as Jupiter rules the muscles, the affliction of Jupiter by the aforesaid influence means rheumatic difficulties, and twitching of the muscles of the lower limbs, caused by Saturn drawing the forces of Jupiter and Mercury toward the sign Cancer, leaving the muscular sign Capricornus negative or without positive polarized force.

Q.—What should be done to prevent difficulties of this kind?

A.—Mercury being in strong aspect to Aries, the sign which signifies speech, desire, *appetite*, indicates that these persons will have very intense and keen appetites. They will like rich food, and good things generally, all of which lands in the stomach, at first. Mars, the fiery planet, is operating upon the stomach. Neptune, just the opposite in effect, also. The two are causing agitation there, and the food passes into the bowels inharmoniously charged, where the natural feverish condition awaits it. The intense appetite overloads the stomach. Hence, the absolute necessity of controlling the appetite, and eating to live. Neptune being a cold, damp magnet, shows that fruits would be pleasing to the stomach, hence their adaptability as food in this case. Mars, the fire planet, indicates warm food, as being good for the stomach, but as the two do not blend, these characters must eat one meal under Neptune and then one under Mars. That is, eat their Neptune meals, and Mars meals at different times. Never mix them. The diet heretofore explained in this work, is here shown to be the best in this case, as sours are needed often.

Q.—What are the business qualifications of these characters?

A.—Mercury is in the physical center or house of business, and being a quick and active magnet, will call them into business life early, and they will become competent in business matters readily, and do well financially. But after middle life they will be drawn by Jupiter and Saturn, which act very much slower, into the realm of the intellectual in life, and they will not care so much for business pursuits. They will make money quick and easy, and although capable business characters, and natural merchants, they are best adapted to the legal and medical professions. They will make excellent teachers, preachers, and lecturers, all of which is the result of Mercury, Jupiter, Saturn and the Earth being strongly polarized to Aries. The mighty Jupiter being in that sign holds and fixes the combination strong and powerful in the head and brain.

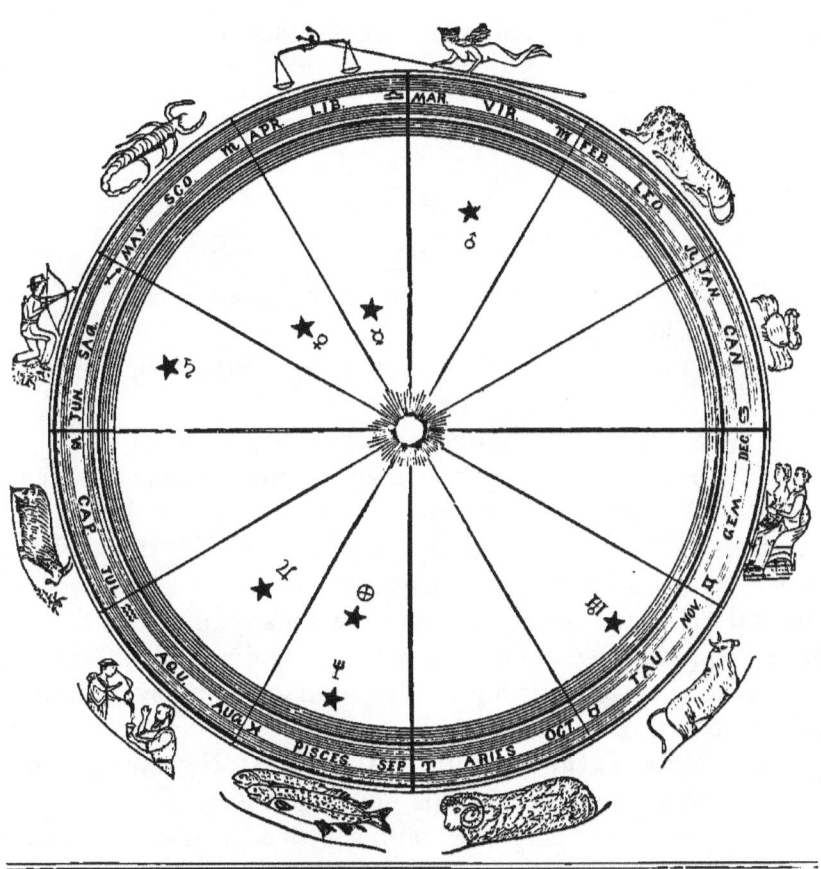

PHYSICAL POWERS.							MENTAL POWERS.						
☿	♀	♂	♃	♄	♅	♆	☿	♀	♂	♃	♄	♅	♆
42	54	51	72	48	54	60	52	67	58	34	73	43	25

DIAGRAM No. 33.

DIAGRAM 33.
QUESTIONS AND ANSWERS.

QUESTION.—In what house is the Earth located in the foregoing wheel of destiny?

ANSWER.—The Earth is in the sign Pisces, in conjunction with the planet Neptune.

Q.—What is the significance of the sign Pisces?

A.—Pisces is the negative sign in the quarter of labor, and also the negative sign in the celestial circle, hence, the Earth is in her most negative position while in this section of her orbit. This shows a strong polarization of the positive forces towards the feet, and causes persons born at this time to be active on the feet, and most always standing or walking if able to be about. This sign indicates a good understanding of things material.

Q.—What is the meaning of the planet Neptune in conjunction with the Earth in this house of Pisces?

A.—Neptune being the magnet which gives one a desire to travel, intensifies the sign effect, and the result is a magnetic condition adapted to traveling over the Earth, especially by land.

Q.—Why by land?

A.—Because Pisces is the most negative house, ana represents negative conditions, and as land is more negative than water, the desires will be for land traveling, instead of by water. When Neptune is in Acquarius or in aspect thereto, the desire will be to travel by water.

Q.—Will persons born at this time ever travel by water?

A.—Persons born at anytime are liable to travel by water? but the above answer shows what the natural uncultivated desire will be of those born under the combination.

Q.—Name the ruling planets in this horoscope.

A.—Jupiter is the physical ruler at 72% of power, and Venus is the mental ruler at 67%.

Q.—Give a full, clear delineation of the planet Jupiter, in connection with this reading.

A.—Jupiter is in the sign Aquarius in third aspect, or juxtaposition to the Earth, and in the vital physical quadrate of the sectional divisions in the nature of our solar system, and in the anatomy of man. Taurus represents the nervous and muscular centers of the system, hence, Jupiter gives strength and power in moderate degree, from his position in Aquarius. The heart sign is more strongly influenced by opposition aspect, which shows muscular strength and healthy action in those parts, which include the heart. Jupiter being in Aquarius, draws all the other forces toward that sign, hence, great capacity for labor is indicated by the single influence of this magnet. The aspect to the Earth and the sign Aries is weak, therefore the mind is operated upon but little, as is shown by the low mental force which is only 34%. This is an indication of a weak mind, with very little will power, and no ambition. Persons thus influenced by Jupiter are easy going, somewhat careless, and negligent, and inclined to be lazy.

Q.—What planets come next in general effect, and what bearing do they have in this combination?

A.—Saturn and Venus are the most important in physical effects, but Saturn being in strongest aspect to the Earth is considered the most important of the two in this delineation. Saturn is in quadrature to the Earth, and in opposition to the house of the lungs, which is a very vital sign when aspected by Saturn, and as Neptune is in conjunction with the Earth, the effect of Neptune upon the lung section is also very strong. The combined forces of Saturn and Neptune aspected so strongly upon the Earth, and the sign Gemini, indicate great danger to the lung section.

Q.—What is the nature of this dangerous indication, and how will these two forces operate to cause trouble?

A.—Neptune is a cold, damp, phlegmatic magnet, which will greatly lower the vibrations of the lung section in persons born under this combination, and produce a condition easily aggravated by other influences. Saturn is the magnet that also causes low vibration and circulation, also stricture of the arteries and veins, the effect of which will be retarded circulation, and lodgement of the impurities of the blood in this weak portion of the system.

Q.—What disease will this be likely to produce?

A.—Consumption.

Q.—Is there no counteracting force that will relieve this bad effect of Saturn and Neptune?

A.—Venus will modify the nature of the disease thus produced, by her aspect to the sign Aries, which will relieve persons suffering from this ailment, of fevers. The positive pole, the brain, will have a harmonious circulation through it, creating harmony instead of fever.

Q.—What other influence does Venus have?

A.—Venus polarized to the brain, to Aries, the sign of expression, indicates tender and sympathetic utterances, but being the mental ruler, she shows us a character easily influenced and led. Not strong in mental force, nor high in intellect.

Q.—We find Uranus, higher in power than Saturn, being

equal to Venus. Why do you not take them up for consideration in their regular order?

A.—The question was, "What planets come next in general effect," and as Saturn is the most important magnet in this case, it was delineated.

Q.—Delineate the planet Uranus.

A.—Uranus is the ruler of the nervous system and is located in the sign Taurus, which is the section of the nerve centers. The force of Uranus is therefore upon the energies, the physical powers, and being in quadrature to Jupiter, unites with him in producing the qualities necessary to a life of trial, and labor. The aspect to the Earth, however, is weak, and the result of these energizing forces is slight. Uranus is weak mentally, so the general effect of Uranus is far below that of Saturn or Venus. Uranus indicates a somewhat nervous temperament, intensified by Mercury in opposition, but slightly modified by Jupiter.

Q.—What is the mental effect of Mars?

A.—Mars has very little positive mental effect, owing to the negative position he occupies in Virgo, the farthest point reached in aphelion. The aspect to the Earth is strong, and the combination of inharmonious vibrations resulting from Neptune in opposition, and Saturn in quadrature, indicate a very disagreeable character to operate with in case of sickness, and a generally bad nature to get along with when well, or apparently so. Mars will give such persons a desire to practice medicine, but Neptune will keep them unsettled, and they will spend a large portion of their time seeking climate, and treatment for their ills.

Q.—What particular effect, if any, does Mars have upon the physical structure of persons born at this time?

A.—Mars is co-ordinated to the alimentary canal and

orifices of the body, and being polarized to Virgo, the section of the stomach, there will be an intense craving for material substances in the shape of food, far beyond the needs of the system. Venus in aspect to Aries indicates that this craving will be for sweets, largely, which will result in a general firing up of the entire system.

Q.—Mercury is the last planet to be considered, and is the lowest in physical power, what does this magnet signify?

A.—Mercury is in Scorpio in quadrature to the sign Leo, the sign of the heart and blood. Mercury rules the blood and circulation, but as Mercury is very weak, only 42%, the vitality, the activity, the capacity to do, and think, and speak, is negative, and without force. Hence, the circulation is easily interfered with. The nervous temperament is intensified somewhat by Mercury in aspect to Taurus, therefore, the general indication of Mercury is, that on account of the lack of vitality, the aforesaid bad combinations have a greater opportunity to depress the system and bring on physical disturbances.

Q.—Has the Moon any particular significance in connection with the planets in this reading?

A.—The Moon is in her new phase, hence the physical polarization is toward the positive or mental nature, which will intensify the Venus expressions and make more feminine the voice and gestures. The physical effect is bad, on account of the strong aspect with Saturn.

Q.—It has been found that these characters are subject to consumption. Is there any way to prevent such a calamity, and is there any mode of treatment which will restore those already partially consumed by this malady?

A.—The nature of the case before us, is one that is seldom treated with any success, for the mind is weak, mulish, and hard to urge into usefulness; and although such minds are easily led, generally, they are all the more stubborn when urged to do the thing necessary to their relief, and they cannot be led away from their appetites. Persons afflicted and partially consumed by this disease, therefore, are very hard to handle, if magnetically stamped at birth with this combination of forces. But if a child is properly understood, and the law of its being fully explained at birth, it is an easy matter to prepare them for a healthy expression, and a generally useful life.

Q.—How would you proceed to train a child born under this horoscope of the heavens?

A.—Appetites are cultivated, principally, and as this combination indicates a desire for sweet food, I would gratify that natural desire by supplying food of that nature which is given us by nature, in a natural way. Such as dates, figs, fruits and nuts. These will produce a beneficial result, while confectionery, and all mixtures, including cake, pie, doughnuts, dressings, puddings, gravys, etc., which these appetites will crave, after being fed on them for a very short time, I should never allow them to even taste of. And as soon as they arrived at an age when they could be taught the effect of such mixtures I would so impress upon the mind the danger of such compounds, that they would never forget it, and with continued lessons in the laws of health and calesthenics, the lungs would never get clogged, they would never be coated and fired up by a mess of pollution, the nature of which is more develish than the lava of Dantes Seventh Hell, and which is the intensifying substance that culminates in the destruction of a section low in action and vitality, but not dangerously so unless aggravated, prodded, abused and neglected, until exhausted.

Q.—Would these persons be obliged to live all through their lives on the food mentioned?

A.—No. Not by any means. The diet mentioned elsewhere in this work, for those who are suffering from this malady, will protect a person through life from this disease. The sweets mentioned were to be used to gratify the natural desire for sweet food.

Q.—What are these characters best adapted for in the business world?

A.—If properly trained they would make good travelers, surveyors, and would have a tendency toward the medical practice, but would not meet with success. They would not be leaders in any line, and wealth would not be made by their efforts. Characters of this nature left to the mercy of an ignorant parentage, would drift from place to place and wind up their earthly existence by succumbing to this dread affliction, consumption.

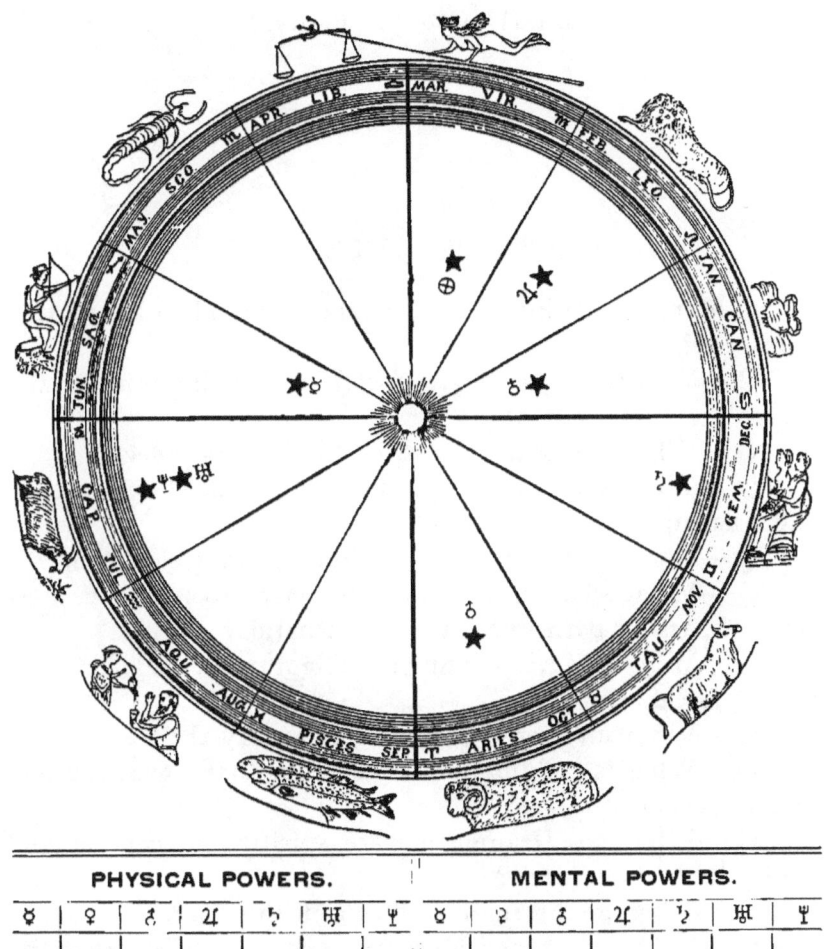

DIAGRAM No. 34.

DIAGRAM 34.
LESSON IN QUESTIONS.

Question.—Why is Venus the physical ruler in this horoscope?

Q.—Why does Venus give a soft and tender tone to the speech?

Q.—Why does Mars run so high in mental effect?

Q.—What is the nature of the effect produced by Mercury and Saturn, upon the Earth?

Q.—Name their aspects to the Earth, and to each other?

Q.—What effect, if any, do they have upon the expressions of persons born under this combination?

Q—.Why is Mars, Uranus and Neptune, a bad combination of forces?

Q.—What magnet is operating to modify their effects?

Q.—What is lacking in this horoscope that would indicate fluent speech?

Q.—Why does Uranus indicate spiritual perception, and ability to read character?

Q.—Why are the thighs afflicted in this combination?

Q.—Does Saturn and Mercury have a bad effect upon the lungs also?

Q.—Why not a serious effect?

Q.—Is the section in which Saturn is located or moving, always less afflicted than the opposite section?

Q.—Why does Jupiter give a healthy heart action, and a generally good circulation throughout the system?

Q.—What effect does Jupiter have upon the muscular and nervous system?

Q.—Why does Mars produce the desire to lead and rule?

Q.—What quality does Saturn give, that indicates leadership, or power to win?

Q.—Delineate each planet separately in this horoscope, and then give their counteracting or strengthening magnets and their combined result.

Q.—What are these characters best adapted to in the business world?

Q.—Why are they builders and jobbers?

Q.—Does Uranus and Neptune always produce characteristics of this nature when in strong aspect to Libra?

Q.—Is it *always* necessary to consider other planets before drawing conclusions?

Q.—Why does the position of the Earth indicate a moral and virtuous nature?

Q.—Why is Venus the physical ruler when Mercury and Saturn are so much stronger in aspect to the Earth?

Q.—The Moon is in her last quarter phase. What effect does she have upon the mental and physical nature?

The foregoing questions have been fully answered, and explained in previous lessons and readings, and students are expected to answer them in their own language from an understanding of the principles, and fixed laws of being, as already set forth. It is far better to be able to answer such questions from an understanding of the fixed principles, than from an understanding of set terms, and phrases, stereotyped for the purpose.

PHYSICAL LIFE.

Physical life originates from a fluid. By the circulation of fluids, physical bodies are formed, increased and supported. One of these life-giving circulating fluids, is the blood.

The body is constantly subject to two distinct processes, viz: decomposition and re-organization. Re-organization is affected by the blood, which, flowing from the heart through the *arteries*, supplies the waste of the system, by restoring decayed parts. The blood in its return to the heart through the *veins*, brings with it those particles which have become deleterious through decomposition. The thinest portion of these deleterious particles pass from the body through the skin in the shape of perspiration; but the grosser particles, that is the more densely related particles, are discharged through the excretaries into the bowels. A want of proper action in these natural drains, is the primary physical cause of all diseases; the first physical symptom. If the natural outlets are closed, the decayed particles or morbid humors must either be retained in the blood, or laid down somewhere within the body. The particular kind of disease which shall ensue, depends altogether on the part wherein these morbid humors may finally be lodged. The same humor, which when lodged in the liver, causes bilious complaints, would, if lodged in the lungs, cause consumption, or, if in the membrane and muscles, rheumatism.

Hence, the magnetic forces charging a human organism at birth determine where the circulation, activity, and harmony, is lacking, and it is in that part of the system thus afflicted that the decaying particles will surely lodge. Therefore, the stars cause the vibrations of our bodies, and by the stars, *and by the stars alone*, can we diagnose diseases correctly.

CAUSE OF DISEASES.

There is but one cause for the diseases afflicting the human family, and that is pollution. There is but one cause for the manifestation resulting from pollution, and that is the action of planetary forces which stamps the human organism with the universal stamp at the time of birth, causing different degrees of activity and circulation, in different parts of the system. The affliction or slow action in vital parts causes them to be more dangerously affected by the pollution above mentioned, than those regions more remote.

WHAT IS POLLUTION?—Pollution is an excess of negative matter taken into the system as food, in combinations and mixtures, incompatible with each other

WHAT IS NEGATIVE MATTER?—Negative matter is food without positive element, life or force.

WHAT DO WE MEAN?—We mean that raised bread, cakes, pie, doughnuts, crackers, biscuits, puddings, beef, pork, mutton, foul, game, fish, and every animal carcass, is negative matter from which pollution alone is the result.

WHY ARE THESE THINGS NEGATIVE?—Simply because the positive or life element has been removed, destroyed or cast out. Take the human organism, something that will bring it home close. When the spirit leaves the body the positive principle is gone, and the negative only remains, and such a mess of pollution is hard to describe.

SHALL WE STARVE?—Yes, that is to say, starve out the the pollution or suffer.

WHAT SHALL WE EAT?—Food that has positive force latent within it, such as potatoes, for instance, they have life, and even when cut in many pieces will sprout and grow and reproduce their kind; food from the vegetable kingdom can be taken into the system with more or less of the positive forces they contain. Nuts and fruits in their natural state, eggs also, have positive force. I feel that some will be saying in their mind, these also have negative substances, which we also take. True. The negative and positive are both taken, but the great point is to take both, instead of casting out the positive, and taking the negative alone. The great desideratum is to balance the system. Balance, even balance, is what we should have, in all things. If these are facts, and no one will know except through experience, they cannot be told. The next thing to be considered is quantity, kind and combinations of such foods as are good for the system. We all eat too much, and thus weaken or overtax our powers of assimilation. We are all environed differently, hence the necessity for variety, and difference in quantity. In the following pages numerous formula are given of various kinds of food, in quantities adapted to different organisms, also courses of diet, for relieving persons suffering from different causes. A strict adherence to the rules and formulas laid down, will more than produce the results herein suggested.

HOW TO EAT.

BREAKFAST.—Omitting the blessing, for reasons which will be explained later, we turn our attention to the evolutions in fruit. Fruit is the best kind of food with which to break a fast, therefore the morning meal should be largely from this class of food. Fruits furnish fluids to the system, and as the fluids of the system are the life elements, after a meal from fruits the system is in excellent condition for a free circulation of the life forces, the expansion of the astral man, as it were, and one is fitted to labor and fulfill the duties of the day, which should be finished by 12 M. The morning meal should be made up from the fruits in season. When berries are ripe, eat berries, and when cherries are ripe, eat cherries, and so on through the season. In the winter the apple is king. The quantity of fruit necessary to be taken at one time depends entirely upon the nature of the person taking the food, and upon the labor, physical, or mental requirements up to the hour of 12 M. A general table of quantities is given below.

NATURAL FOOD FOR BREAKFAST.—One ordinary apple, one-half pound of grapes, one-quarter pound of cherries, berries or plums, one or two good pears, two peaches, one orange, one banana, half a pound of raisins with figs. Melons in season.

Any one of the above is sufficient for people who do not perform physical labor, no matter who they are. I have tested them for years both from choice, *and necessity*, and I know I am right when I say the amounts named are sufficient and abundant for strength and health.

The above amounts may be increased by those who do physical labor, even to double the amount if necessary, as many times is the case with those who labor, causing the system to throw off fluids freely through the pores, in perspiration. The fact that such food can be easily digested, assimilated and thrown off, is the very reason it is best to take into the system before performing physical or even mental labor.

THINK WHEN YOU ARE EATING.—Consider the wonderful production before you, ask from whence it came, and by what means it has been brought to its present wonderful beauty and perfection. Talk to the food before you, in your mind, and you will find that through the greatest kindness, care, protection, admiration and love, it has been evolved and lifted into a condition of harmony suitable to be incorporated into the elements composing the grandest structure upon the globe, man.

WHAT DO WE EAT FOR?—This question should ever be in mind when food is taken into the system. Is it because we like the feeling on the end of our tongue, the tickling of the palate, the stretching of the stomach, and clogging of the bowels that we gorge ourselves, and then rush for a pipe or take a chew of tobacco, in order to aid digestion and get more tongue and palate tickle? Is it tickle alone we are seeking?

WE SHOULD EAT TO LIVE.—And those of the Orient, who were able to prolong their lives to several hundred years, done so through a system of diet, from which the positive elements and forces alone were transmuted, thus adding strength and power to the system from day to day.

DINNER.—We have now completed the days labor, that is to say, we should do all labor from 8 to 12. This is not the practice at the present time, *but it will be the practice in coming time.* The Sun is at high meridian, let us pray. Why pray? Because the Sun is at high meridian, and it is the only time to pray and expect the best results, and all should do this before they dine. What has the Sun got to do with our prayers? Everything to do with them, as no person can pray and receive benefit except through the Sun, and every theologian, every religious worshipper, and every person on the globe to-day, that doubles themselves in what they term an attitude of prayer, do so because they don't know any better, therefore, are not to be blamed. Many are sincere and honest, many are not.

SO LET US PRAY.—And how shall we pray? No one is qualified to pray unless they know how, and why they do so, and are so situated that it is possible to do so scientifically and intelligently. I lived thirty-five years before I ever bowed my head in prayer, during those years I learned how, I reasoned out the meaning of prayer, and I went at it the first time intelligently and fearlessly, and found that it was good for me, and good for every one, so I decided to illustrate it in this work, so that all who need the uplifting and beneficial influence of prayer, can drink at the central fountain and realize on the spot that their supplication has been taken notice of and answered, by the great ruler of our system. At the base of the brain at the back of the head and neck is located the central station of the nervous system, (see explanations of the sign Taurus) being the center of the nervous system it is the most sensitive spot, physically, of the system. Whenever anything afflicts this section, whether planetary influence or the influence of the immediate surroundings, such for instance, as the weather, or the dampness of a room in which one is sometimes placed, or a draft from a window, this vital center becomes inactive to a degree, and a physical disturbance is produced. This being the case, the protection of these parts on all occasions is necessary. Hence, the covering of the same with clothing, first by nature, with long hair, secondly, or later, by the substitution or partial substitute of clothing, leaving sufficient opening or nakedness to jeopardize the health, however. But to protect these parts clothing is used to keep the parts warm, for by keeping them at a certain temperature the nerves are in a condition to respond to the mind and will, and vivify and make possible the expression of thought. This being the case, how can we pray so as to receive strength and benefit from the Sun.

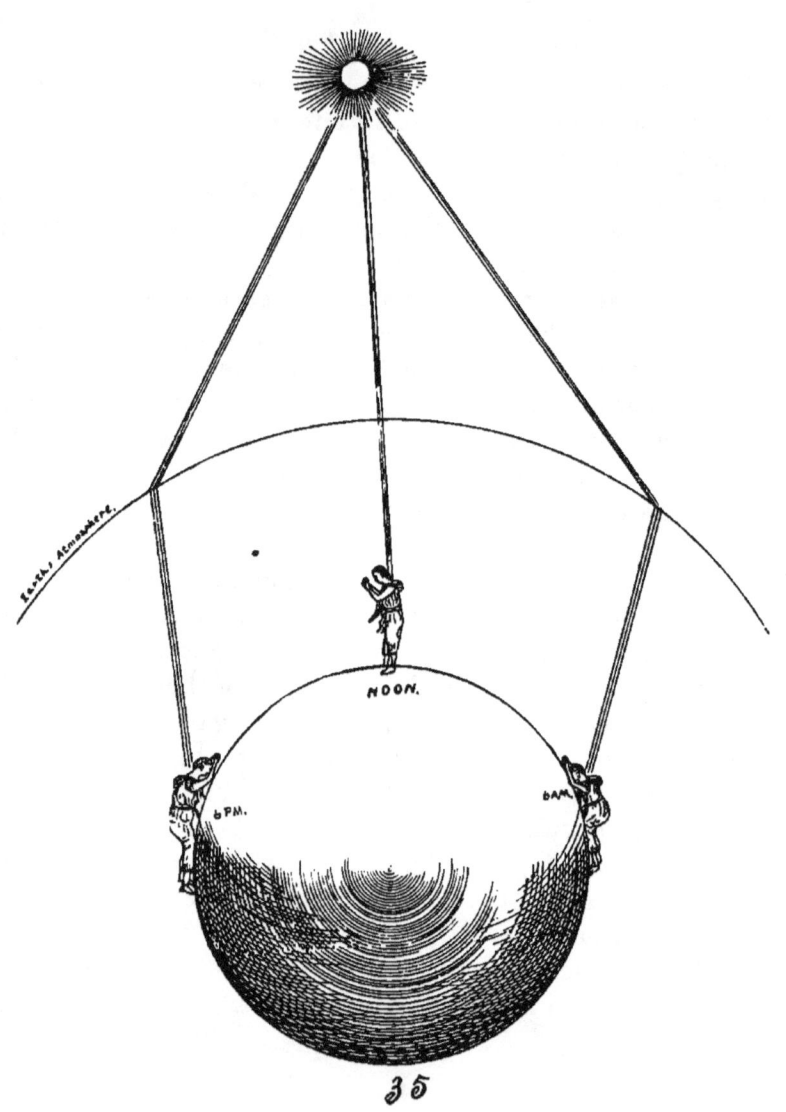

DIAGRAM 35.
PRAYER ILLUSTRATED.

At high meridian the Sun is at its highest point over head and the rays of light come more direct to the side of the Earth nearest the Sun, than at any other time during its revolution upon its axis, producing a stronger and more positive force to penetrate into, and vivify physical bodies. At such times, by standing or kneeling as is most convenient, bowing the head slightly to shade the eyes, and to form an angle so that the rays from the Sun will strike directly on the top and back part of the head, neck, and down the spinal column. The warming and vivifying rays direct from the center of our solar system and from such a strong and powerful magnet as the Sun, which is nearly 900,000 miles in diameter, pulsating through 95,000,000 miles of ether at the rate of 186,000 miles per second, have an effect upon the physical constitution of man, that all should experience and understand. The foregoing diagram shows the rays of the Sun at high meridian with the Earth and man in position for prayer, also shows the angle of the Sun's rays at morning and evening. Hence, the necessity of bowing the head to the ground at such times in order to receive the most benefit. This may explain to the unprejudiced some of the so-called heathen customs of the Sun worshippers of old. Some may argue that it is best to stand with the back to the Sun, and also ask why it is necessary to fold the hands and raise them before the face as shown in cut. The reason is reasonable and scientific. If one goes to a concert they wish to face the music, they can receive the vibrations better; they are in a natural position to receive something. The same with prayer. Through the hands and the fingers we give out most of our strength. Magnetism, as it is called. During the labor of the day the blood is actively operating through the arms and hands. We are giving off strength and power then. When the work is done and the strength has been reduced, before partaking of the mid-day meal we should renew our forces, calm and pacify our nervous system. So in prayer the hands should be raised, allowing the blood to settle back, return to the heart, and other parts, and by placing the hands, or better still, the palms and fingers together, the outgoing currents of magnetism are connected and mostly retained in the body. So that by fulfilling all of the requirements suggested herein the very best receptive and negative condition is produced, in which great good, both physical and mental may come.

WHAT SHALL WE SAY?—This seems to be the next question that comes up. As all this praying is purely a physical manifestation and pertains to the anatomy of man, it is best to keep the mouth closed, for we give off force and power by talking. In place of saying something, think over your physical body and find any weak places that may exist, concentrate upon that weakness, and the vivifying influence may be more intensely exerted upon those parts, raising the vibratory activities, and intensifying the life therein.

IS THIS THE ONLY WAY TO PRAY.—There is *one* other way, and it has been explained, and definitely stated, and repeatedly stated. It is only necessary to call attention to the sayings of Jesus. Retire into your closet, and in silence commune with the holy spirit. This is spiritual communion in reality, and like physical prayer should be silent, without speech.

Thought, desire, receptivity, and soul recognition alone are required, in either case. Every invalid will be greatly benefitted by a half hour prayer of either kind. Both should be indulged in by those who are heavy laden, and are seeking rest, and an altar of prayer should be upon every house-top, for the worship of the Sun.

Having made ready for the mid-day meal, we will explain what is best to take into the system at such a time. It is the warmest part of the day, the system has been warmed by the forenoon labor, (or should have been) the noon-day prayer has also warmed and vivified the system. As the law of affinity produces harmony, why should we not continue this harmonious blending and eat a good warm meal. The mid-day meal should be warm, and the products of the field and garden, the foods to be softened by fire, to render them palatable. The potato is king of the vegetable kingdom, the beet, parsnip, turnip, squash, cabbage, carrot, etc., etc., come along in their order, and in preparing should be steamed or baked, for best results; because by steaming they are surrounded on all sides at once with heat which holds within all of the finer flavors and juices. Vegetable food should be eaten as plain as possible, a little salt only is needed. Dressings and stuffings are packey and indigestible mixtures, or elements inharmoniously blended. The quantity and kinds to be eaten together, must be regulated according to expenditure of force, and the following amounts may be increased to meet the requirements.

DINNERS FIT FOR THE GODS.

One fair sized potato, an ordinary side dish of turnips, squash, cabbage or other vegetable, only one at a meal, with warm unleavened bread, made by stirring graham flour and cold water into a thin batter, with a little salt added if desired, and baked 40 minutes in a hot oven. A little rice may be eaten for dessert. This is sufficient. The above is a diet for restoring health, and if to restore health, why not for general use?

A FEAST.—Potatoes, parsnips, green peas, unleavened bread and baked apples, is a combination for a mid-day meal that a king might look upon with pleasure.

[NOTE.—Some argue that vegetables contain earthy matter in greater degree than fruits and nuts, therefore are unfit for food. But it seems to me that as the entire vegetable product—in present form, as well as nearly all fruits, and nuts, are the result of the genius of man, recognizing the universal reward for labor, to those who work in the gardens of the gods. For it is by recognizing the Infinite law and acting harmoniously with it, that it is possible to improve, evolve, and perfect any of the natural products of the Earth. The method being harmonious and in accord with the divine or highest law known, the result of such transmutation from the dust, should be good for man. Therefore, I hold that all of the products of the earth which *nature yields to the hand of man without resistance*, is good for food if used in proper quantities, and at proper times.]

After the mid-day meal no work or active expression, either physical or mental should be entered into, at least for an hour or two, until the system has had time to assimilate the food. The afternoon should be spent in social recreation, and amusement, in exchange of ideas, out among the fields and flowers, or if in winter, in the house by the grate. At six the evening meal should be eaten, and should consist of nuts and dates, which co-ordinate and harmonize beautifully with each other and they seem to belong together; soaked wheat may be eaten at this time also. One-half pound nuts before cracking, or one-quarter pound of meats and one-half pound of dates, is sufficient for a meal, or one-half teacup of soaked wheat and a few raisins makes an excellent evening meal, (the amount may be increased, same as in other formulas mentioned.) In case one is going out in the evening it is better to eat some fruit, say an apple, banana, a few grapes, pears, or peaches, something to give quick and active expression, but if one is to retire at the usual hour, the nuts, etc., first mentioned are best.

WHY?—Because it is the nature of nuts, raisins, cereals

and dried fruits, to retire, concentrate, draw in and rest. Wheat is able to rest the longest and yet is able to reproduce its kind. On account of their nature they fit the system best when resting and inbreathing from the universe, preparatory for a new days experiences. Fruits are expressive and quick, just the opposite of nuts and wheat. Hence, the difference in time of using them. Nut meats contain a greater proportion of positive life force according to bulk than any other food. The cereals come next. The cereals are the best for food, generally speaking, because the positive or life element responds, expresses many times quicker than that of nuts. You place a kernel of wheat in the ground and it bursts forth in a few hours, while a nut requires several weeks to make ready for expression. They are both excellent food. Wheat being the king of all products for generating life, force, power, strength, health and harmony in human organisms, we place it at the head as king; and the best way to prepare wheat for the quickest and best results is to soak it in clear water for ten hours. It should then be eaten raw. Eaten slowly and thoroughly masticated. The effect of wheat thus prepared and eaten, has the same effect, apparently, in giving power, strength, mind force, etc., that the planet Jupiter has in magnetic effect upon physical organisms at birth, showing conclusively that wheat is co-ordinated to Jupiter, magnetically. Hence, the great mistake has been made by some writers, in considering this relationship, that wheat was brought here from the planet Jupiter, originally. It is just as reasonable to suppose that every human organism strongly influenced by Venus, was brought here from that planet. The fact is, all the products of the Earth are the result of magnetic or planetary influence, and every plant and tree, as well as every species of animal, have ruling planets, or magnets, the same as human organisms.

35-

DIAGRAM 35—
A WORD TO THE SEEKER.

The symbolism of the Zodiac in its relation to man, (see diagram 35—) shows how the body is polarized to the spiritual, mental and physical significations of the houses. For instance, note the position of the organism during formation, as shown in diagram 4, all above the solar plexus is on the mental side, then observe that the feet and limbs remain the same, symbolically, and the balance of the figure straightens up, throwing, the entire frame upon the physical side of the Zodiac. This places the head of the physical man at Libra, the physical sign, showing that the physical expression must come first, to all.

The majority of the human race never get back on to the mental side of the scale, but live upon the physical plane through life. Some, however, seek a higher realm, and to such this lesson is given.

When the few get tired of physical experiences, and seek to know something of the deeper realities of their natures they reach out toward the mental and spiritual side of life. In doing this they become meek and lowly. They bow the head as if in prayer. They yearn for something. They seek. As they bow the head in a passive, negative, humble manner, the brain crosses the upper celestial meridian symbolically, and enters the sign Virgo. The brain receives this vibration and it dawns upon the intellect that virtue is the first requisite necessary to attainment.

The planets move from the mental signs to the right, passing into the physical sign at Libra, so the seeker must remember that in order to attain power it is necessary to look up the stream and travel contrary to the natural physical tendencies.

Virtue, then seems to be the first and all important requirement for mental and spiritual attainment. It is the Rock of Ages upon which rests the powers of the adept. When firmly established upon this rock, powers undreamed of begin to develope, and the sign Leo is reached in due time. With greater power comes more potent thought, and Cancer signifies mental activity and concentration. With these attainments come a power for harmony, and the quarter of love, affinity is entered into in the sign Gemini.

This being a quadratic section to the house or sign of virtue, the strength is here tested before the sign of energy, and power over physical things is entered. If able to stand the test, Taurus gives the greatest physical power possible. And with this power knowledge comes, and with knowledge the sign Aries, the sign of intuition, perception, inspiration, and individuality and positiveness is reached. In attaining this degree of unfoldment one becomes qualified to give utterance from the wisdom of the soul, which vibrates in unison with the highest and holiest that the children of Earth can know. When one thus attains and closes the circle by bringing the positive and negative principles together again, the condition of childhood, and simplicity is reached, a condition of perfect peace and trust and happiness. In this condition the ways of the Infinite are made clear, and all wisdom is with the life eternal that dwells within. With this attainment the human body is transformed into an instrument, or medium for the highest.

Individual determination and effort can bring this about, nothing else. All physical appetites and desires must be controlled first. All become metaphysical healers and teachers, who accomplish this.

The real significance of this lesson must be perceived. It cannot be taught.

INDIVIDUAL ASTRAL VIBRATION.

Our physical bodies are made up from the dust of the Earth, and from conception to birth, and from birth to death, everything outside of our bodies is vibrating toward it. We are operated upon from without, by everything about us, most potent of which are the planets of our solar system. It has been explained that if Mercury is in strong aspect to the Earth at birth, that the circulation, the vibration, the activities, are greater than when Mercury is in weak aspect. This being the law, it is plain to be seen that a soul when embodied is capable of vibrating the astral fluid of which it is composed, and penetrating through the physical body, according to the physical or magnetic stamp at birth. This is the natural uncultivated condition, and relation of the astral to the physical.

DIAGRAMS 36–37.

The soul vibrates from within outward. The following diagrams will illustrate the power of an astral, under different magnetic physical environments. Diagrams No. 36 and 37 show the natural action of the astral vibrations, meeting the magnetic or planetary forces. Or to state it more clearly, the action of the astral or interior forces within a body whose magnetic or planetary condition is produced by the horoscope shown in this illustration.

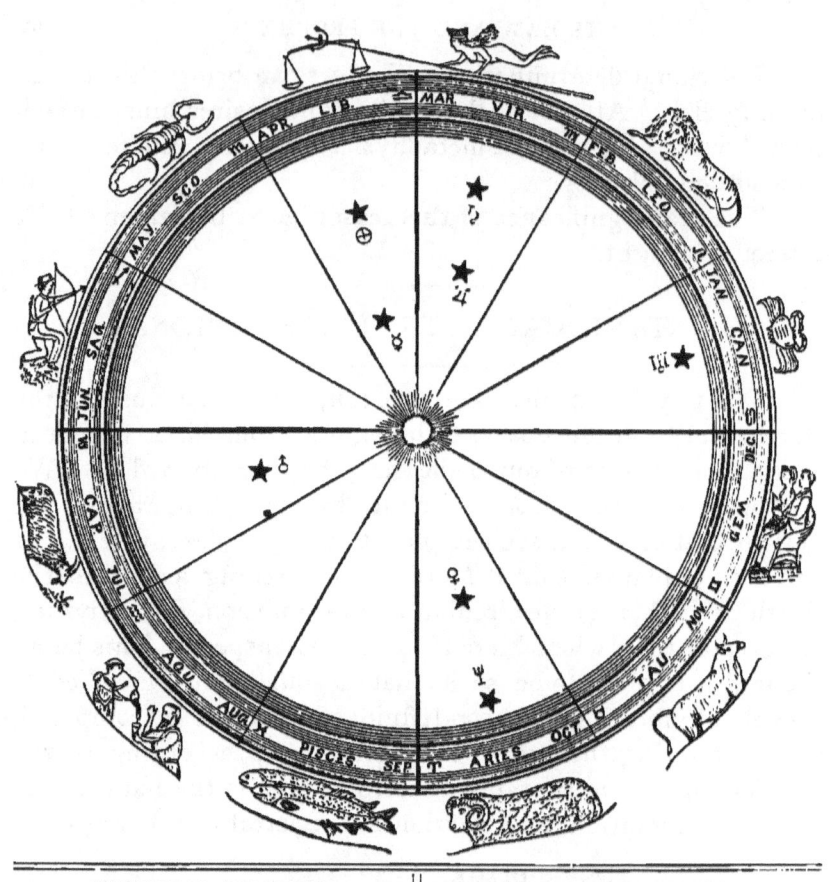

PHYSICAL POWERS.								MENTAL POWERS.					
☿	♀	♂	♃	♄	♅	♆	☿	♀	♂	♃	♄	♅	♆

DIAGRAM No. 36.

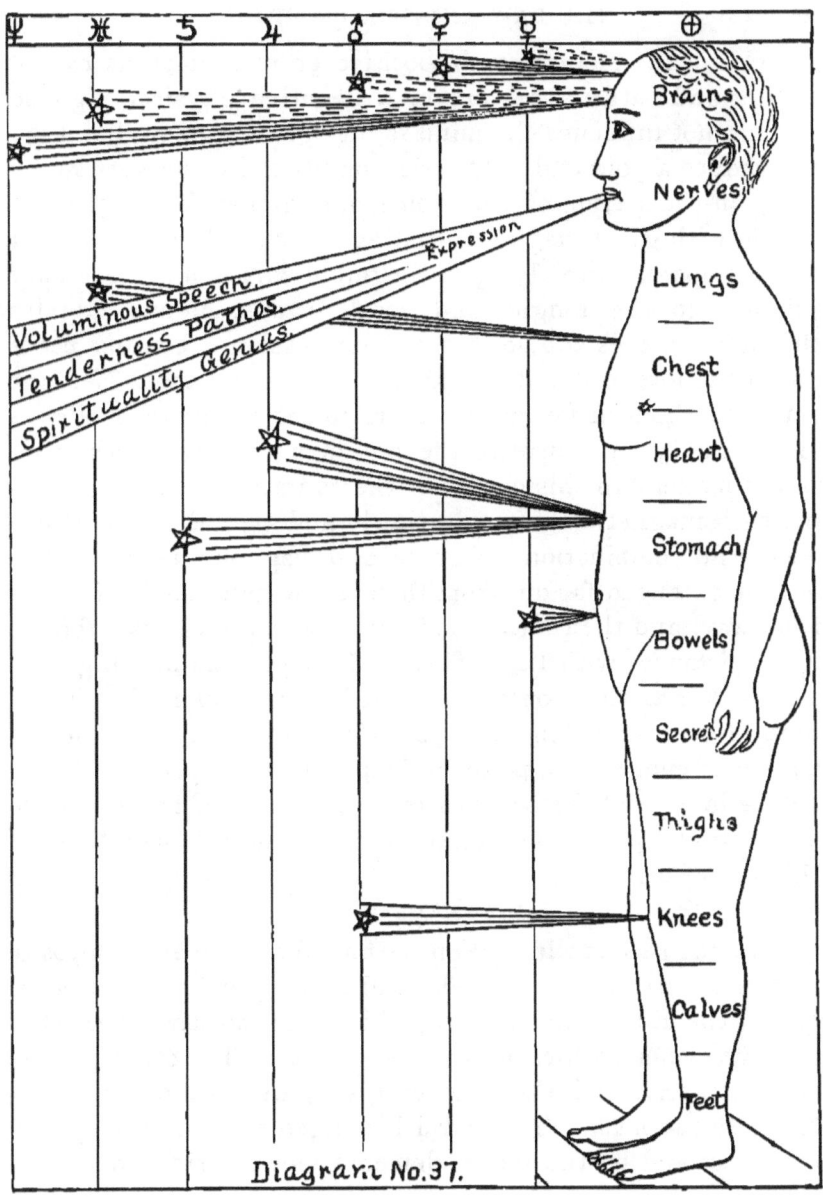

Diagram No. 37.

All of the planets are in positive or mental signs except Jupiter and Saturn; they are in a negative physical sign, so they do not influence the mind to any great extent; but they do produce a powerful magnetic condition in the system by being in the section of the stomach, and therefore indicate a person with great magnetic healing gifts. All of the other planets operate directly upon the mind and brain. Mercury vibrates to the tongue and vocal organs; Venus vibrates through the eyes and softens the expression. Uranus peeps out of the forehead and investigates things spiritual. Neptune leads the thought far away. Mars comes out between Venus and Mercury, and corrects the blunders that they otherwise would make. In this character the vibrations are very forcible both magnetically, or physically and mentally. This is a wonderful combination for mental and magnetic healing. The aura is extended far out from the system and can be felt ten feet away, and the thought is very potent, and can be vibrated great distances with little effort. Many persons meeting such a character as this would be stunned for a moment by the vibrant forces so potent and powerful. By study and concentration of energy, the power to be gained by a person of this nature is beyond the belief or comprehension of those who do not seek and prove to themselves the wonderful operations of this law of being.

DIAGRAMS 38–39.

In the second illustration we find almost an exact opposite as far as forces are concerned. All of the planets are negative except the Earth and Saturn, which are positive upon the nervous system, which means a weakness. The other planets being negative and Mercury being very weak there is nothing to vivify the flesh. The astral is obliged to vivify the system or retreat and let the outer elements slowly grind them into

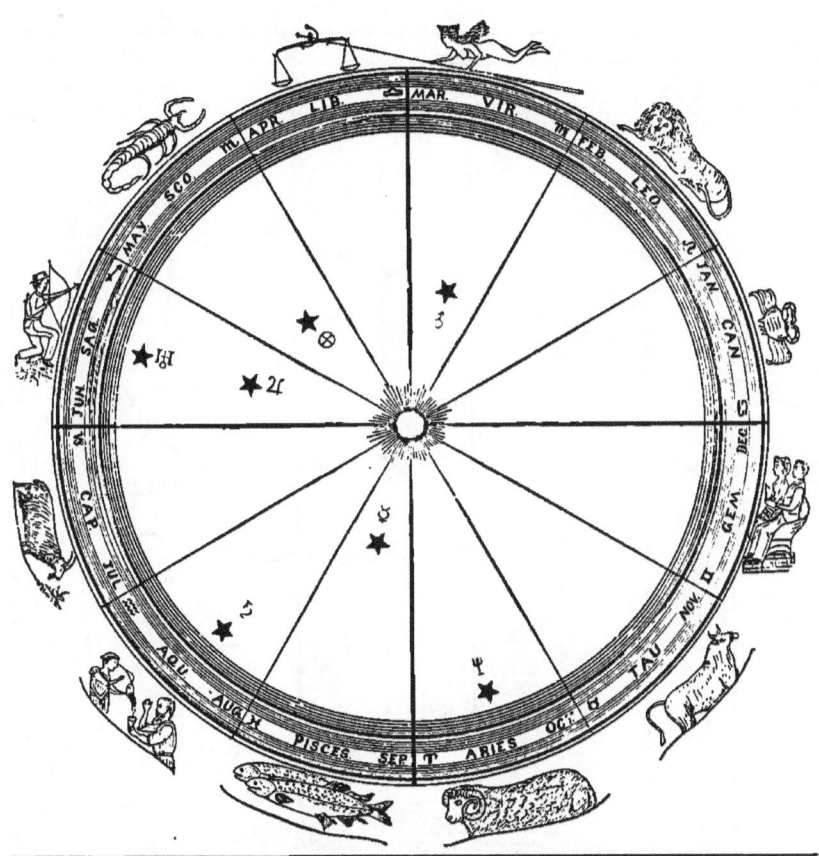

PHYSICAL POWERS.							MENTAL POWERS.						
☿	♀	♂	♃	♄	♅	♆	☿	♀	♂	♃	♄	♅	♆

DIAGRAM No. 38.

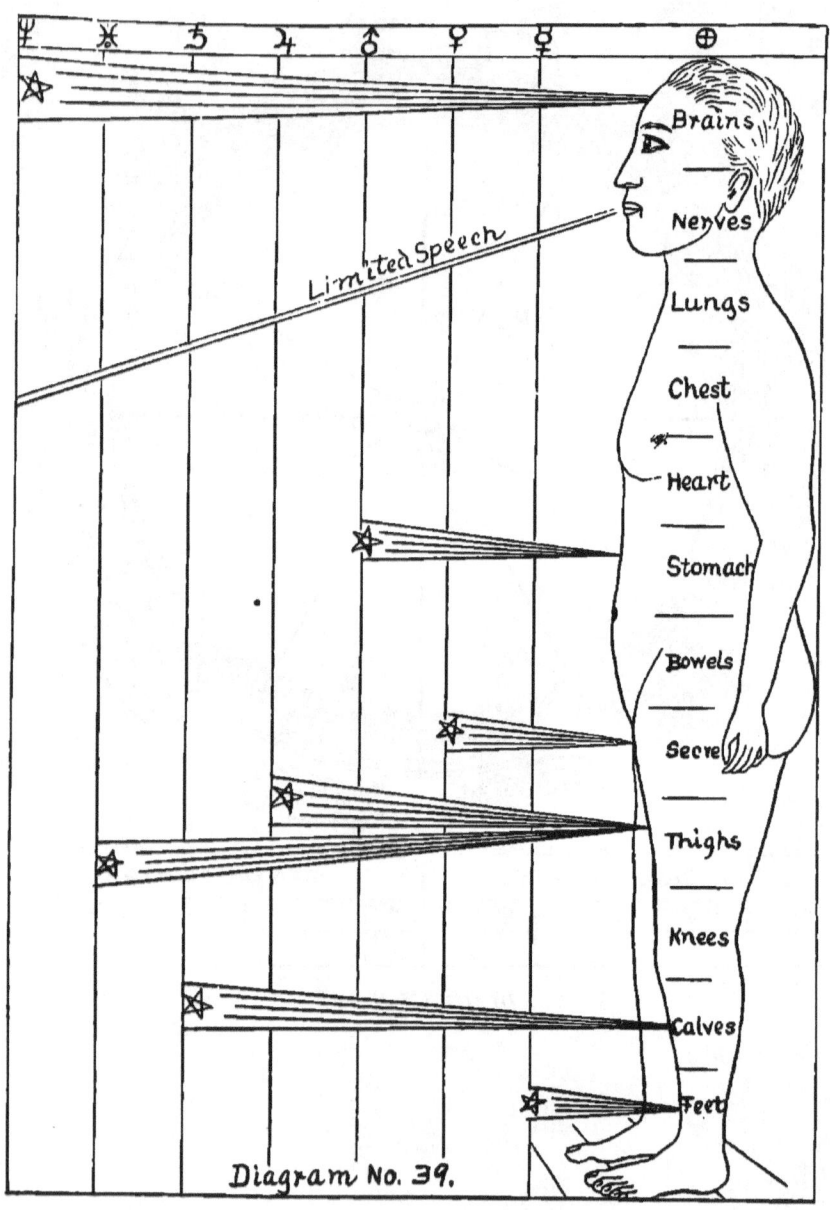

Diagram No. 39.

the dust. Neptune alone influences the mind and the yearning produced is for something out of reach. These characters will always want, and never have anything, and never accomplish anything. Their souls cannot penetrate, and vivify the body, and they have no brains or mental qualities to appeal to. Everything is dormant, cloddy, stiff, and disagreeable.

DIAGRAMS 40–41.

In this combination we have a wonderful physical balance, but a very negative expression from the physical. The vitality is low on account of Mercury being in weak aspect to the Earth. The conjunctions make a very enduring physical constitution. Mercury alone, operates upon the mind, the sign Aries, the section of speech and expression. This wonderful balance of the planets will produce a sensation of satisfaction within, and a high appreciation of self. But Mercury has no governor, therefore the utterances will be silly, flighty, without sense, and very untruthful. The whole life will be spent bragging about self, and what self can do. Such persons will never accomplish anything worthy of mention, but will sit for days and talk about little insignificant personal matters.

We will change two planets and give this character some brains to back up what Mercury can express when it is there to express.

DIAGRAMS 43–44.

By this change of Jupiter and the Earth into the house of Libra, we produce a character with great mental power, giving Mercury something to express. Jupiter being the planet of wealth, will cause this mind to seek wealth and large business dealings on account of being in the trade house with the Earth in conjunction. This means millions to this char-

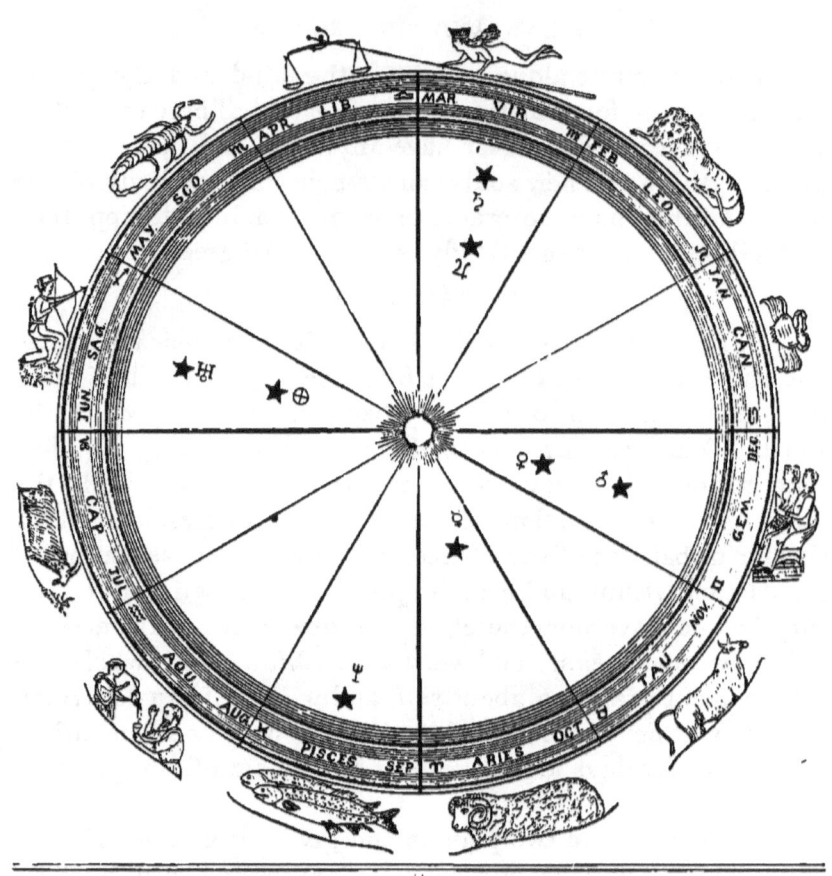

PHYSICAL POWERS.							MENTAL POWERS.						
☿	♀	♂	♃	♄	♅	♆	☿	♀	♂	♃	♄	♅	♆

DIAGRAM No. 40.

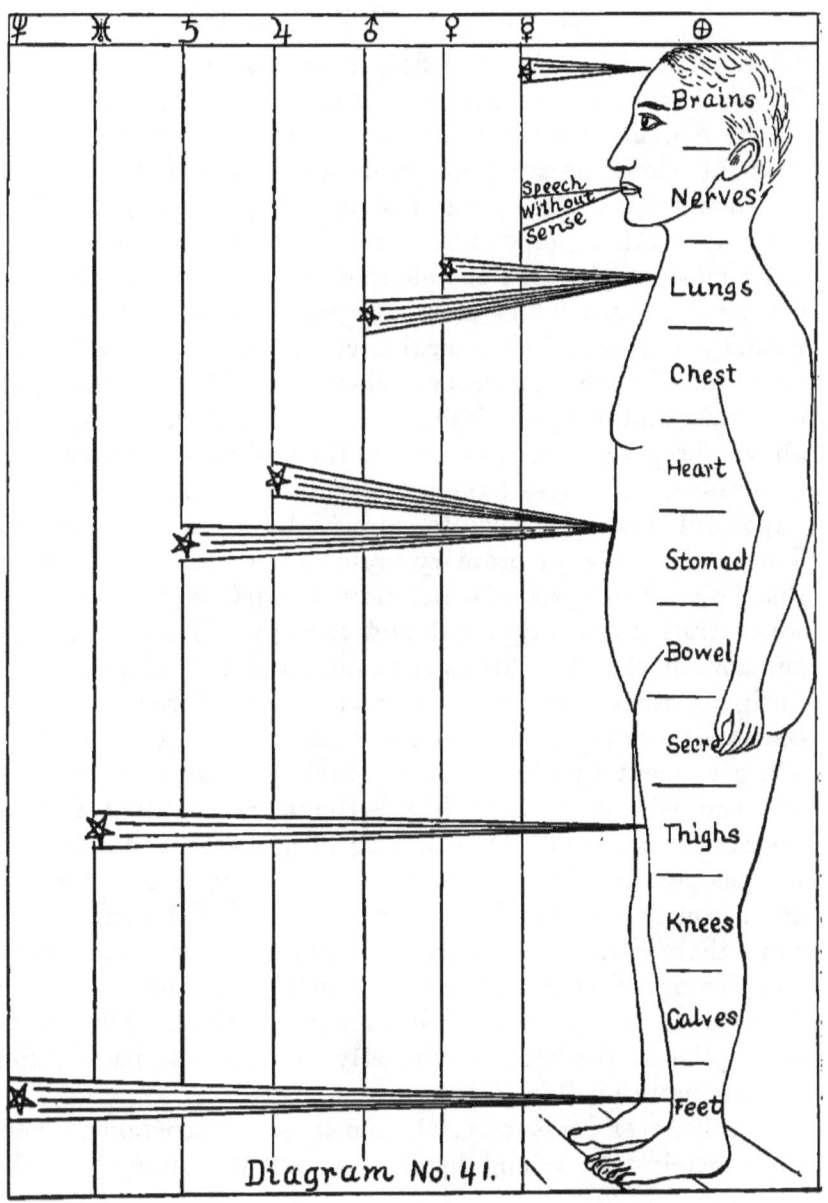

Diagram No. 41.

acter, for wealth will surely flow to such in great abundance. Physical vibrations extend but a short distance, that is they can be sensed but a short distance from the body. Mental or thought vibrations are more potent and subtle, and can be directed and transmitted great distances, repeating their vibrations upon others, producing sensations and effects undreamed of by most people. To be able to do this and to build about ourselves an aura which cannot be penetrated or contaminated, means power over the physical environment of the flesh. To this end, all should strive, and when all are thus protected, all may meet and mingle without fear, and without danger, for all will be pure, clean, and true to the highest and holiest that is possible. To vibrate the astral substance then, is the all important lesson we wish to convey by these illustrations. Those who have an ordinary brain can cultivate and produce that force or will power, which nature failed to give them, by concentration of energy, will and thought. Take a subject, and confine the thoughts to the same, and continue to do so until no other subject can attract the mind from it. Then take another subject, and do the same thing. This exercise will give mental power. For physical exercise in concentrating the vibrant forces within—the astral substance—take breathing exercises. Draw a long, deep breath, and hold it as long as possible, expanding the entire body, vivifying every atom from the crown of the head to the sole of the feet. Continue these exercises until you can start the perspiration from any section of your body at any time by concentrating your forces upon that portion of the anatomy. When this can be accomplished, the battle is virtually won, and the possibilities of your nature will be determined.

Whenever you sneeze, which means you have taken a cold, immediately take a long breath, (we should always breathe through the nose, not the mouth,) and hold it until the entire system is vibrated, and strained somewhat. The chill will be thrown off at once, and no cold will be experienced. There must be no delay in this, it must be done at once.

Do not sit around and wait for some spirit to come and do your work, and heal your infirmities. You are embodied for the purpose of expressing your own spirit, see to it that no one robs you of the right. Receive all of the good vibrations that spirits can give you, but do something for yourself, if you expect results.

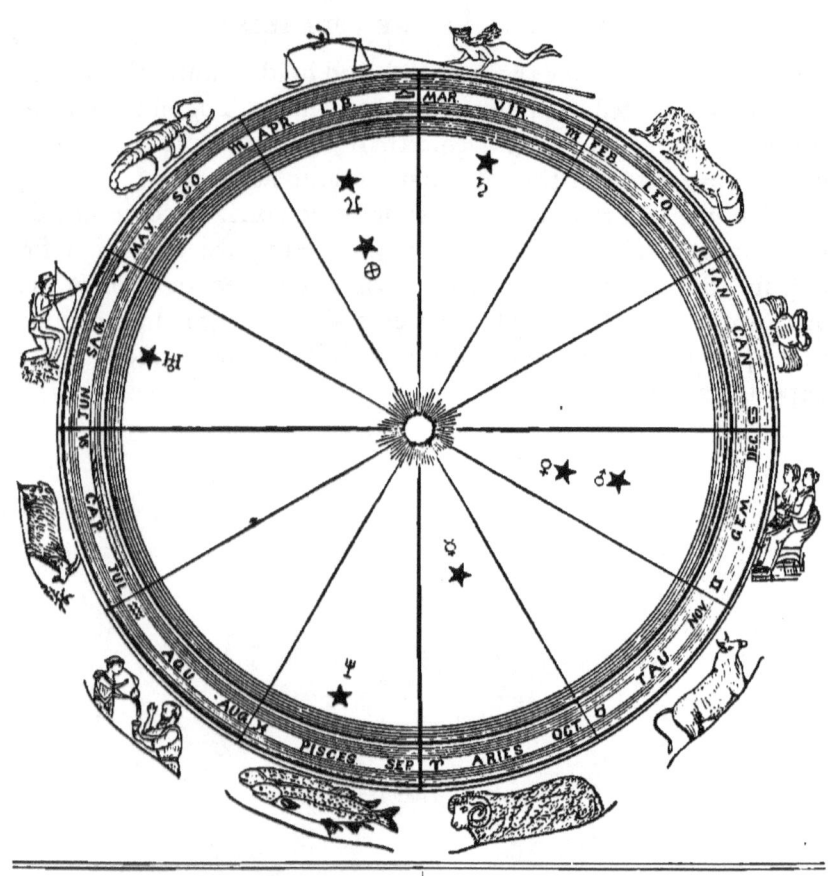

PHYSICAL POWERS.							MENTAL POWERS.						
☿	♀	♂	♃	♄	♅	♆	☿	♀	♂	♃	♄	♅	♆

DIAGRAM No. 43.

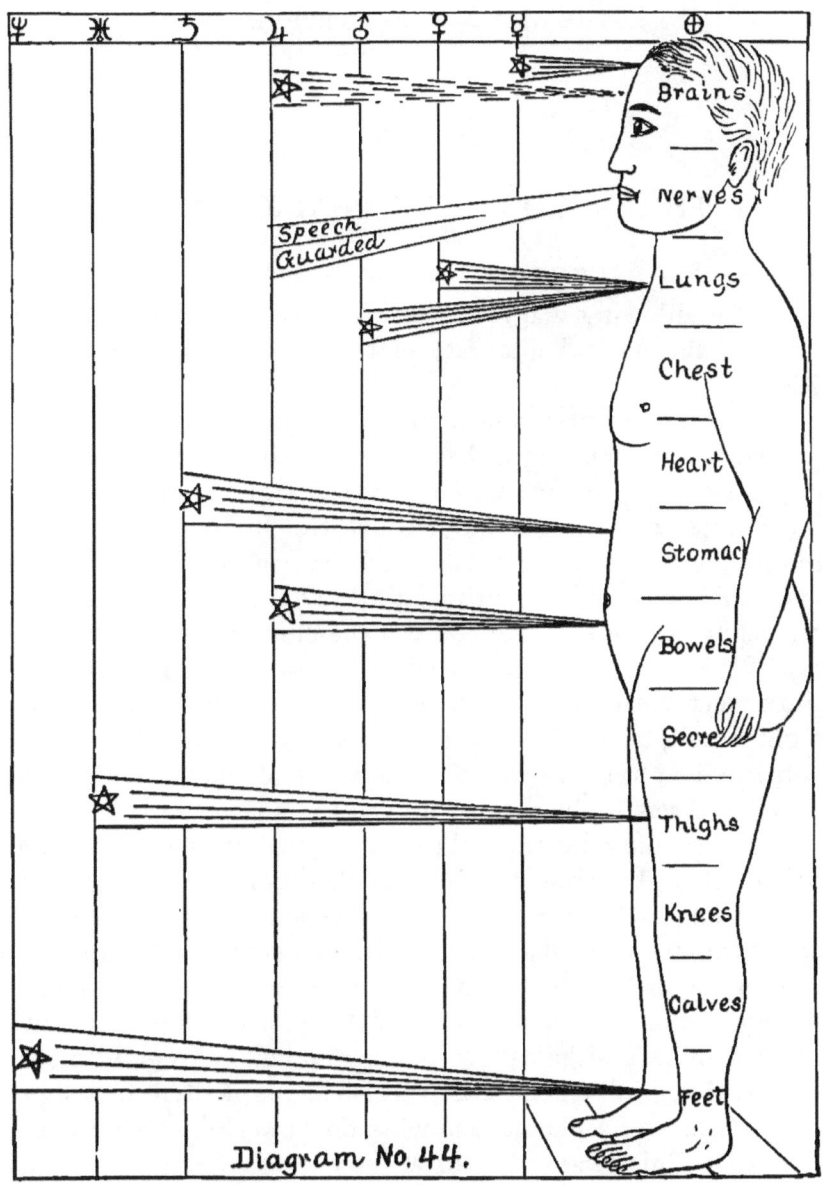

Diagram No. 44.

PHRENOLOGY AND PHYSIOGNOMY.

THE MENTAL QUADRATE.

The following diagram illustrates the phrenological sections of the mental quadrate of the houses or signs of the Zodiac.

Aries comes first, and includes the physiognomy. When planets are in this sign, they intensify intuition, perception, impression, clairvoyant vision, physical sight, smell and taste. They draw to this sign, and focalize the influence of planets in other sections of the Zodiac, and thus intensify the powers and functions covered by this sign. This phrenological quarter begins at the extreme point of the chin and extends to the top of the forehead, as indicated in diagram. These four sections meet at the drum of the ear, where sound, not sensed by sight, smell, or taste, vibrates from every quarter of the universe and appeals to the consciousness of man at this focal center. Aries is the mental sign in the quarter of love

Cancer includes the bulk of the upper brain, or cerebrum, hence, thought, consideration, deliberation, study, research, calculation, determination, form, system and direction, are qualifications, or traits, indicated by planets when in the sign Cancer, according to the nature of each. Cancer is a very brainy section, the mental sign in the quarter of wisdom, and planets in this sign denote power and ability to gain knowledge easily. When the Earth is also in one of these four signs the influence of a planet is much more powerful, as already explained. This section begins at the end of Aries and extends

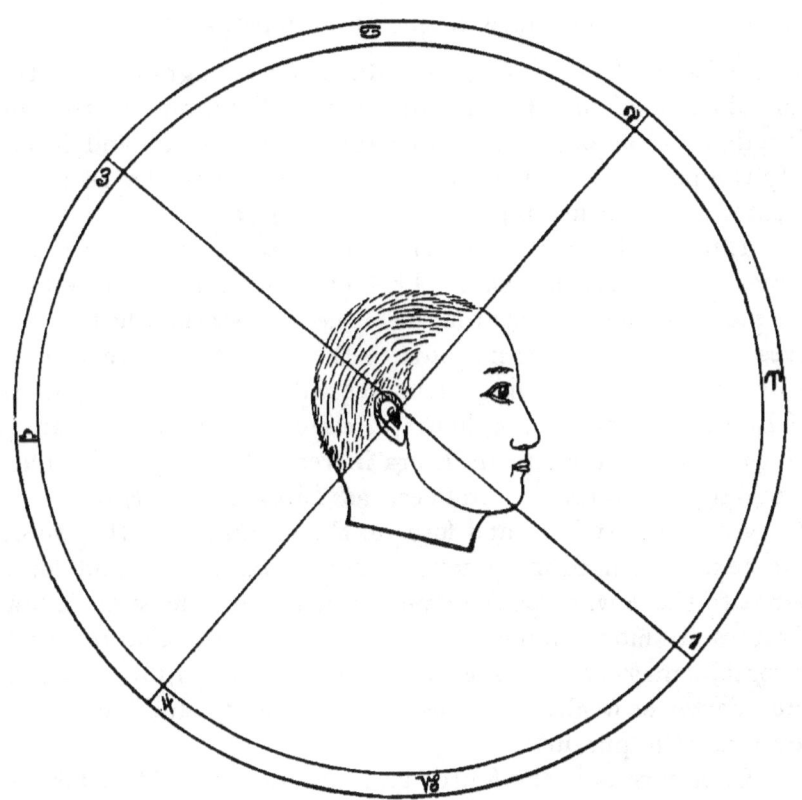

to the back of the brain, as indicated in diagram. As the convolutions of the brain in this section direct and control the functions of the organism; to be able to single out and intensify the power of each functional brain center is the secret to mental power in healing, and influencing others.

Libra is that section in which is centered the powers and forces of the physical man. The cerebelum and nerve centers are stationed here, and through this central station the thought fires up, as it were, for its journey through the different parts of the system. In giving utterance with the lips the powers of Libra are drawn upon, hence, the significance of the planets in that sign. Planets in Libra increase the physical forces, especially in verbal utterances, as Libra is opposite Aries. They furnish backing and force to the meaning of the words and sentences used in speech. They furnish nerve and confidence to those who speak in public, when in the sign Libra. Orators are more competent when Libra is well charged with favorable magnets for speech and eloquence. Libra being in the quarter of wealth signifies business ability, and inclination to mercantile pursuits.

Capricornus is the fourth and last section in the mental quadrate, and covers the muscular centers of strength and powers of all human physical bodies, from a phrenological standpoint. This section is opposite the sign Cancer and signifies power and ability mentally to execute upon the physical or business plane. When this sign has powerful magnets like Jupiter, Saturn, Neptune or Uranus, they signify ability to carry on enterprises according to the nature of the planet. Jupiter signifying power to make money in such labors, while Saturn signifies power to do, but trouble in doing, and financial loss. Neptune means gain and financial success. Uranus means inventive genius and ability to accomplish much in carrying forward business projects, but with little financial gain. Capricornus is the mental sign in the quarter of labor, and signifies strong and powerful characters when well charged by powerful magnets.

This mental quadrate must be consulted in order to find the capabilities of persons intellectually, and especially as to their powers for giving utterance, expression, and explanation of their views. There are no public speakers worth listening to who have no planets in this mental quadrate at birth. The planets that give the greatest possibilities in this quadrate are Mercury, which gives fluency in speech, quick and potent thoughts, high perception, vivid imagination, wit, mirth, and vitality. The next best magnet for intelligence and oratorical qualifications is Mars, which gives calculation, accuracy, force, declaration, argument, and seriousness. Mercury and Mars together in this quadrate with the Earth, gives a most intense mental nature, and the greatest conversationalist possible to be produced. The next best magnet is Jupiter, which adds strength and majesty to the character, and force, power and eloquence to the expression. With these three magnets should be placed the planet Venus next in order to improve the conditions, as Venus gives pathos, tenderness and harmony to speech and gesture. Saturn, Uranus, and Neptune come along in their order after the others as arranged and explained. There are many combinations, however, which give great mental power when in this quadrate, Jupiter, Saturn, and the Earth, or Saturn, Neptune and the Earth, or Jupiter, Mercury and Uranus and Venus, Mercury and Saturn are not bad combinations. The bad combinations are: Mars, Mercury and Saturn; Mars, Mercury and Uranus; Uranus and Saturn; Mars and Saturn; Mercury and Saturn; Mercury and Neptune. The horrible combinations are: Mercury, Mars, Jupiter,

Saturn; Mercury, Uranus, Mars and Saturn; Uranus, Neptune, Mars and Saturn; Mercury, Mars and Uranus.

Whenever these bad combinations come in the mental quadrate, they signify that the mind is in a bad state, and the causes should be fully explained to those who seek relief, for they will be much more contented with a knowledge of the cause of their inward feelings, than they will in ignorance of it.

These good and bad combinations effect people in a similar manner when they come in the vital or mental quadrates; but the mentality is more intensely operated upon in the mental signs. A bad combination acting upon the nervous system, deranges the system, and the mind is effected by the sustenance taken through the physical or nerve centers to supply the brain.

The full Phrenological Zodiac is given herein showing the divisions of the head and the influence upon the mental, and anatomical development of the cranium.

Aries covers that portion which includes the sense of smell and taste, and signifies those qualifications and desires as explained or written in that division. When Mercury, the planet of keenest sense, because the most vital, is in this section, these senses are made very keen. The nose and chin is sharpened also in shape, if no large magnets are in the mental quadrate, to thicken these parts. When Saturn is in this section the senses are dull, negative, and subject to irritation.. Inharmony afflicts the speech, and a generally bad expression is the result. Place Venus in this section and the appetite is increased and the desire for material things, stimulants and odors is also intensified. The utterances are rendered harmonious and soft, however.

Mars makes harsh the utterances, but precision in expressing ideas, and so all of the planets operate according to their

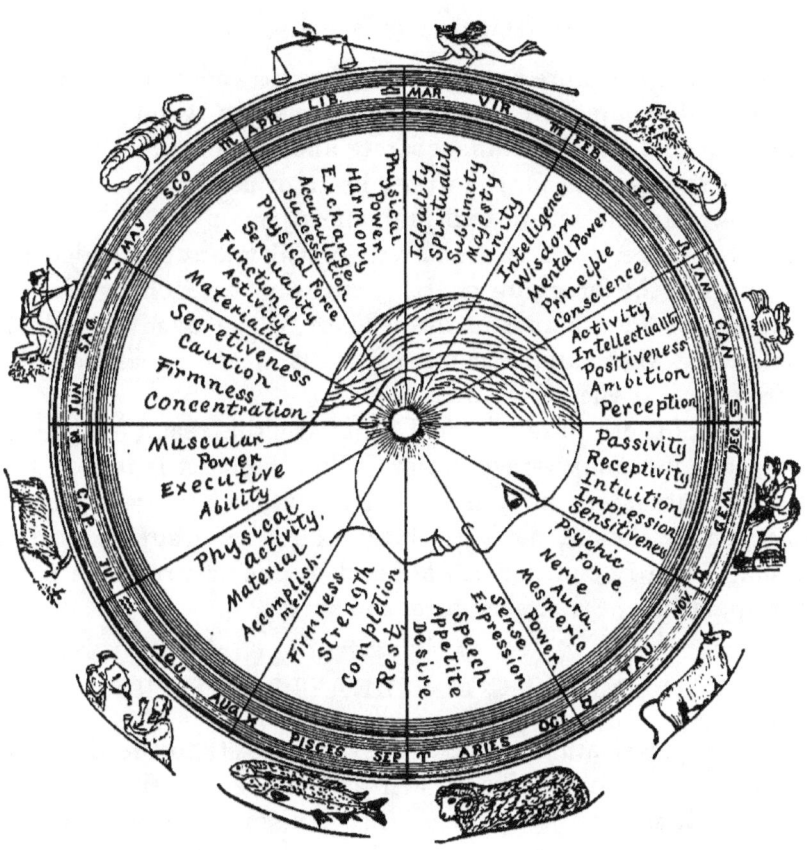

natures, as heretofore explained in physical and mental delineations. The object of this explanation is to show how the planets effect the cranium, separate and distinct from the balance of the system, for the upper brain or cerebrum, manifests the power latent within each human organism.

Remember each of the phrenological traits or tendencies as given in the foregoing chart, or diagram, in each sign, is intensified by each planet in the sign, or in the quadrate which includes a sign, and when a planet is weak in aspect, the phrenological effect is limited.

All of these phrenological traits are the result of physiological conditions, for example: When a planet is in Leo, the blood is intensified in action, the heart is made more powerful in its action, hence, the brain receives a greater supply, and it is magnetically charged at the heart by the nature of the magnet operating in that section or quadrate.

MAGNETIC CO-ORDINATION CHART.

The polarization of the heavenly magnets to the different sections in the anatomies of men and women, is the cause of the harmony, or otherwise, that exists between married couples, and in fact, the cause of harmony and inharmony in human life generally. The following diagrams will show harmonious and inharmonious unions. As all unions are more or less inharmonious, it is only necessary to illustrate the reason for it without attempting to offer a remedy, except to those who are yet to be united. Wherever this chart shows cross currents of planets that do not harmonize or blend, on those lines inharmony creeps in, and wherever these lines meet and are agreeable magnetically on such lines, harmony blesses the union. Thus Mercury and Neptune can never cross each other. Venus and Uranus, Saturn and Mars meet also and blend mentally and physically, while Jupiter is the center and signifies wealth, power and glory on which most people agree to get all they can of, so Jupiter is the ruler of the Earth, and its partnership relations. The broken lines show the action of planets in the mental quadrate outside of Aries, intensifying the mental powers.

The illustration which indicates harmony, shows a perfect meeting of the physical vibrations of the two organisms. Jupiter, Uranus, and Neptune is operating upon the mind of the male, which signifies few words, but deep and intense thought, calculation and understanding. The female brain is operated upon by Mercury, Venus and Jupiter, showing a fluency of speech, harmonious and pathetic.

The illustration of inharmonious co-ordinations, shows no physical cross currents or inharmony, but the cross currents of Neptune, Uranus and Mars, from the male brain, conflict with Neptune and Saturn in the female. The Neptune vibrations from each harmonize all right, and also the Mars from the male, and Saturn from the female, but the male head has Uranus operating also which does not blend with either Saturn or Mars, hence, contention on the mental plane, causing jealousy and distrust..

[This chart is copyrighted, but will be furnished to those using this work at a reasonable figure, in connection with a blank certificate of the Law of Being, arranged for full mental and physical delineations according to the rules herein explained]

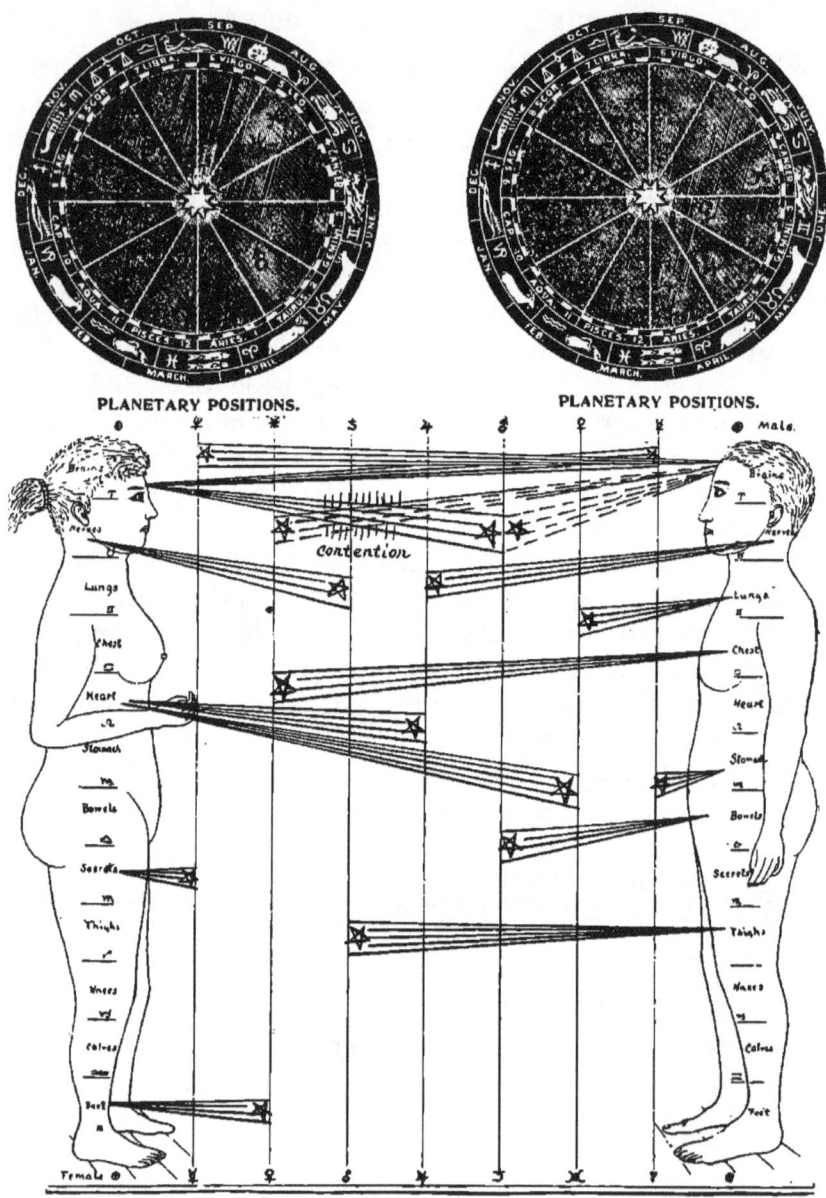

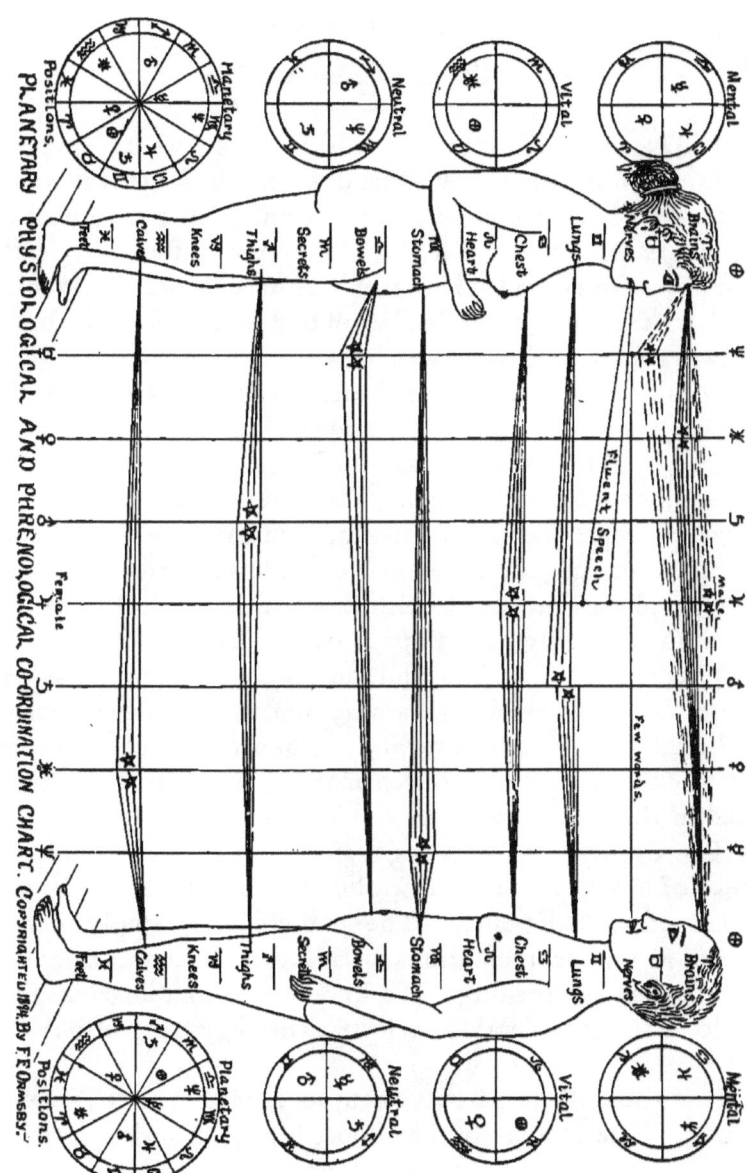

AN IDEAL CHARACTER.

The closing illustration in this work shows a horoscope (diagram 45) of the heavens most favorable for entrance into mortal life. Diagram 46 shows the result when favorable environments are found. An ideal character, gifted physically, mentally, morally, and spiritually. A natural orator, a genius, a worker, a teacher, and a leader among men. Such a character always goes to the front and makes his mark in the world. He needs no guardian, he needs no teacher; his soul is harmoniously related to the material world. Such natures may be produced by the genius of man. Who is there, that would not be proud of such a son as this. The careless, loose, accidental, haphazard, reproduction of our kind renders it almost impossible for souls to gain a favorable entrance into mortal life. Most people are afraid to think on this subject, therefore misery and suffering are rampant on the Earth.

This work, "The Law and the Prophets," is for those who wish to use it in an educational way, not for the idler who reads that he may satisfy his curiosity. The world needs the information it contains, and we need more of the characters represented in this illustration.

The Chinese figure the age of a person from conception instead of birth, which is all right with an understanding of the law of embodiments. The planets are rapidly changing, and forming combinations, both favorable and unfavorable, for the primal proceeding. To know these combinations, is to be able to select a suitable period for the beginning of physical life.

It is the duty of parents then, to consult the "Tables of the Law," The Oracles of the "most high," in order to raise a gifted, intelligent, healthy, and happy family.

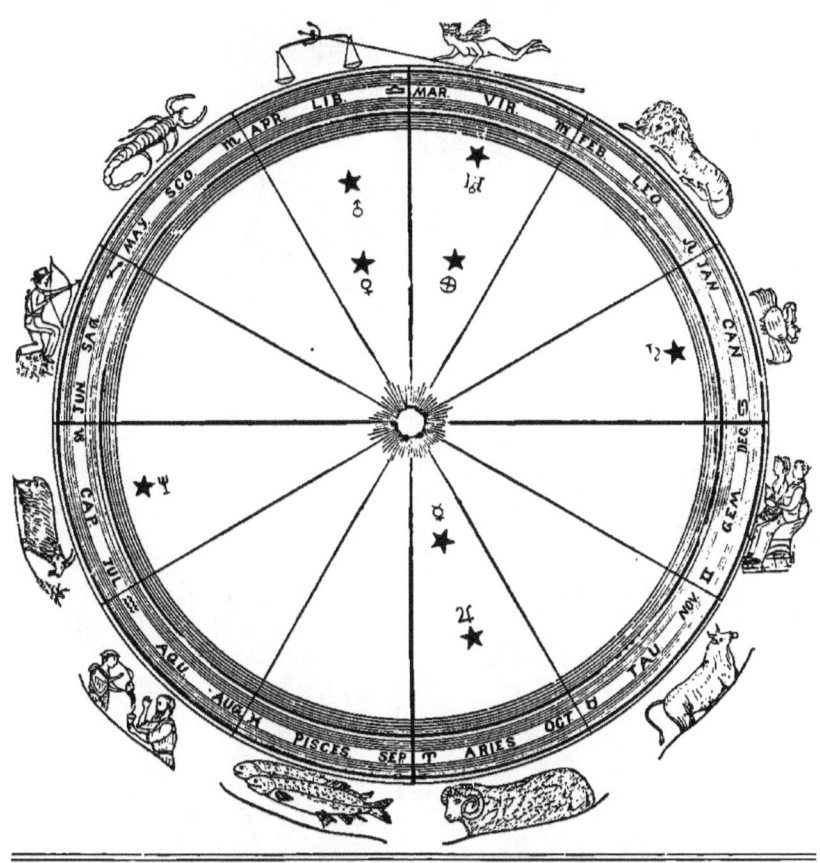

DIAGRAM No. 45.

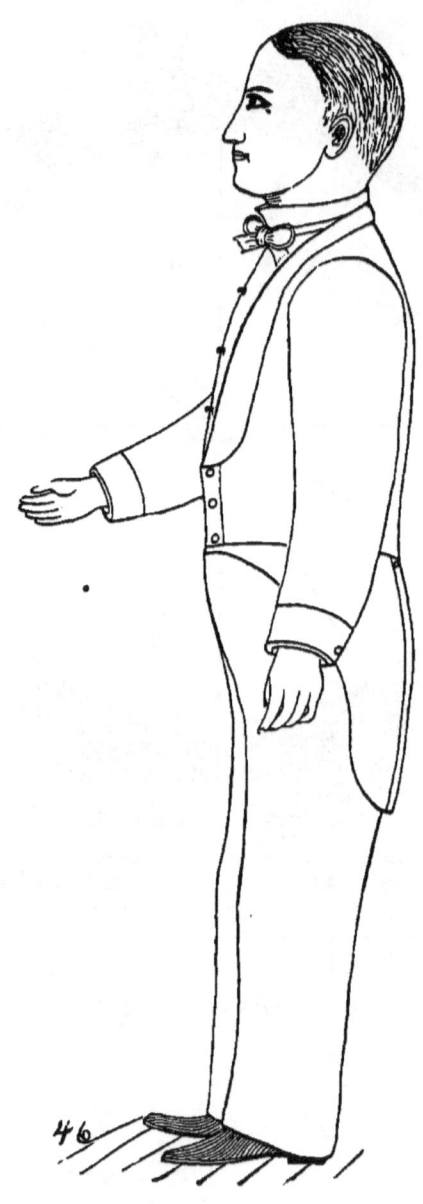

INCARNATIONS.

It is plain to be seen that material expressions in nature are evolutionary. The fruits and flowers of the garden declare it; the breeding of stock declares it. The wonderful physical development of the Grecian and Roman nations proves conclusively that great strides in the evolution of human species have been, and may be made. Therefore, it behooves us to know something of the processes by which these things are accomplished.

As the magnetic law has such an important bearing upon the powers and capabilities of persons born into the world, our first duty is to study and understand this law, and to this end, this work is written.

It is hoped that all who purchase a copy of this book will immediately form a class, and go to teaching this law. They should not wait until they have mastered it themselves, for the subject is an Infinite one. It is better to form a class at once and get some help to elucidate the subject. Souls are seeking for a favorable earthly environment. Those souls best learned in the law, can choose the best conditions generally. But there is so little choice in conditions that it is almost useless to seek. Of course the higher and holier the aspirations and capabilities of the parents, the higher and holier the nature of souls they attract to them. Hence, great souls usually embody with mothers who are honorable, upright and true to themselves, though they may not be stylish, eloquent or even refined, according to the social standard. An honest, upright, pure minded woman, therefore, is the first primal requisite.

The more learned the better, because in the training and education of an offspring, learning is very necessary, but if both honesty and learning cannot be found in one person, honesty is by far the most desirable.

The next requisite is a proper mate, a man who is magnetically co-ordinated and spiritually conditioned and enlightened. With such a union, the most favorable physical preparations are made. The next thing is to be able to read the stars and Moon and find when there is a desirable combination of magnetic forces, for remember, the more intelligence and genius displayed in building a physical organism, the greater will be the production, the same as writing a book or making a watch.

With an understanding of these laws, as set forth in this work, and the above suggestions, I will leave the subject for those who are to prepare the way for coming generations, trusting that in the year 2180 or thereabouts, when I return to embody again, there will be so many invitations extended to me from those learned in "THE LAW AND THE PROPHETS," that I will be able to find veritable Angels in human guise, ready to welcome me, and call me by name.

The Rocky Mountains will be my place of landing in that prophetic century, when Mystics from the Orient and the Occident will bring to the Earth a new dawn, by their advent among the people of that section of country, which is to be the grandest and most beautiful the world has ever known.

THE ADEPT.

As the positive forces are the highest when the Earth enters the sign Aries, that portion of the Earth nearest the equator, is best for the expression of positiveness, therefore, best for the development of mind force, and mental power.

Hence, for ages, the greatest of all mental and psychic powers have been evolved through the lives of those born in Egypt, Persia, India, and other countries near the equator. Those born at just the right time, say about September 25th, December 25th, March 23d, or June 24th, are those whose development and wisdom outrivals the world in matters occult. They are the adepts, the masters, the prophets, the seers and interpreters of the "sacred word," and revealers of the hidden laws, and forces, permeating the entire universe. They stand above the common herd, and are worshipped by those who cannot "read their titles clear to mansions in the sky." And yet they are only greater expressions of the possibilities of each.

The positions of the planets on the dates given determine the degree of power of those who are born when the Earth enters one of these four signs. There may be stronger combinations for positiveness on other dates, therefore, it must not be supposed that bright and positive minds cannot be produced at other times. But if the planets are in powerful aspect for mental and will power, and the Earth is in one of the four houses mentioned, the direct effect upon the Earth is greatly intensified and a more positive relation and result is produced. With this natural magnetic condition must come experiences, which will unfold the latent possibilities of the nature, until the higher mental and spiritual (especially the latter) powers are made manifest, understood, and brought under the subjection of the *will*. To accomplish this, is the all in all of human life and development.

SPIRITUALLY.

Let those who seek this higher goal,
    Drink deep, or not at all,
Lest they become entangled,
    And through the senses fall.

Remember, all must earn their way,
    All alone the journey take,
And from the pure waters of life
    Their unquenched thirst must slake.

And as they seek in outer world,
    Where'er the mental part would lead,
Experiences thus are gained,
    Most valuable indeed.

Another realm they'll surely find,
    In which all wisdom lies;
Within their souls a mystic key
    Unlocks the starry skies.

The Infinite plan is there made plain,
    And in the silence of the night,
Angels from that higher realm,
    Reveal the "Hidden Light."

The light that makes for man on Earth
    A heaven where'er he dwells;
Brings music of the vibrant spheres;
    The chimes of starry bells.

It gives to him who seeks aright,
    Inspiration and power divine;
To understand all outward forms,
    And penetrate the inner shrine

Of embodied souls, and spirits gone,
    Of worlds and systems yet to be,
Of all that is, or e'er has been,
    In the boundless cycle of Infinity.

This sacred light is a "Word" of might,
    And "*Man*" its counterpart on Earth,
Must drink at its fountain, pure and bright,
    Before he wins the higher birth.

The hidden fire must consume the dross,
    The healing waters soothe the pain,
And Mother Earth must claim her own,
    Ere we mount the airy heights again.

TABLES.

The tables giving the powers of the different planets in the twelve houses or divisions of the Zodiac when correctly calculated as to their relation to the Earth, and her power of position, according to rule, shows two ruling stars, a physical ruler and a mental ruler. The physical ruler is the planet strongest in power according to the physical table, while the mental ruler is the strongest in effect upon the mind.

There is still another ruling star which is by far the most potent of all in the complete career of a life, and that is the planet in strongest aspect to the Earth, regardless of percentages. This is called the life ruler, and explains the general nature and character. The physical ruler, therefore pertains to the physical body, the mental ruler to the mentality, while the life ruler pertains to the general proceedings, impulses and desires.

The tables for placing the planets together with the mechanical chart is the result of much study, experiment, and mathematical calculation, and required the making of over eleven hundred thousand figures to simplify and bring it to its present state of usefulness. By this simple device, and a table with one correction annually, the positions of the planets of our solar system may be found for any day, for all time, past, present and future; making it a perpetual ephemeris for all time. The simplicity of its construction brings it within the comprehension of children, and also simplifies the study of the stars from an occult standpoint, so that each and every one may soon know their meaning, and be able to read character, and delineate physical conditions without difficulty.

MECHANICAL CHART AND TABLES.

The mechanical chart and tables are used as follows: The outer circles printed on the bed piece of chart gives the days of the month, month of the year, and the day that the Earth enters each sign. Every other date is given in figures, the two days being divided by a small line, to avoid small figures. A slate or tablet of paper may be used on which to mark the circle, signs and divisions of the Zodiac.

Now, suppose we wish to find what signs the planets were in when baby Esther was born, September 9th, 1893. First find what sign the Earth was in on that date, by tracing the date circle to September 9th, and observing what sign is in the circle outside of said date. We find it is Pisces, so the Earth should be placed in the sign Pisces on the slate. It will be observed that the Earth entered Pisces on August 23d, hence is in that sign until September 24th.

The revolving disk represents Mercury, Venus, Mars and the Moon, by colored circles and divisions for each.

The green circle represents Mercury.

The blue circle represents Venus.

The red circle represents Mars.

The center circle represents the Moon.

The disk must be set according to tables for the year under consideration for each planet, in order to find its position.

To find Mercury we refer to table for setting the disk of the chart, and run down the column giving the years at the left, until we come to 1893, and for the year 1893 we find that Mercury entered the sign Scorpio, on January 7th. Have disk right side up. We now turn the disk toward the bottom with the right hand until the first sign of Scorpio, on green circle, we come to is at January 7th. The line dividing Libra from Scorpio should be even with line dividing January 6th from January 7th. Hold in place and run the sight around the circle to September 9th, and the sign Leo will be on the green circle on disk opposite that date. In the Zodiac this is the house or sign for Mercury only, on that date. So we place Mercury in the sign Leo.

It will be seen at once that when this disk is set according to the table any year, that any date may be found for that year without moving the disk. The same with the other planets (except as explained concerning the Black Star.)

We find in the table 1893, that Venus entered Scorpio on January 2d. Always have the disk right side up to start with. Draw down with the right hand as with Mercury until the sign Scorpio is at January 2d. Now, by following the Venus or blue circle around the disk, we come to the end of the circle indicated by the black star, which is at the end of the sign Libra. Observe the date line opposite the line denoting the end of Libra, which is August 14th, and turn the disk toward you with the right hand to the beginning of the coming sign, which is Scorpio. That is to say, so that the beginning of Scorpio will be on the line beginning August 14th. Refer as before to September 9th, and we find the sign Sagittarius opposite on the *blue circle*, so we place Venus in that sign on the slate.

Mars has two circles, as that planet moves only one-half the distance around the Zodiac each year. It is in reality a continuous circle. On February 5th, 1893, Mars entered Gemini according to table, set the same as others, and on September 9th, the sign Virgo is on the *red circle*, so we place Mars in the sign Virgo on the slate.

The first new Moon in 1893, we find in table to be on January 16th, set in same manner, and on September 9th, it is a new Moon. Place the Moon always in the same sign with the Earth—new Moon between the Earth and Sun, full Moon opposite, and the quarters at right angels thereto.

After the disk has been set and the sign found for the date desired, for one planet, it is not necessary to pay any attention to that circle when finding the next one. A straight edge may be used from center to outer circle or date to set disk true, if necessary, when they are close to lines. The four outer planets are found in tables without using the chart as they remain a long time in each sign.

We now refer to table of Jupiter, and we find that planet entered Taurus on January 20th, 1893. As Jupiter remains in each sign about one year, of course on September 9th, he is still in Taurus. Saturn, Uranus, and Neptune, are found in like manner.

Saturn remains in each sign about two and one-half years, Uranus seven, and Neptune fourteen years. Having placed all of the planets on the slate in their proper signs for September 9th, 1893, we have produced a horoscope of the heavens at the birth of Miss Esther Cleveland, Washington, D. C. (These simple rules should be well learned, as they apply to all dates.)

★ THE BLACK STAR.

On each circle of the revolving disk is a Black Star denoting the end. Whenever it is necessary to pass this star after the disk has been set, in order to arrive at the date figured on, we must observe the date of the end, and turn the disk back to the following sign, and then proceed to date desired. The sign then opposite on the disk will be correct.

EXAMPLE.—Suppose Mercury enters Aries on January 1st, any year, then set Aries at January 1st. Now, suppose the date figured on is December 28th, in passing around the circle we pass the Black Star on the Mercury circle before we reach December 28th, so we must take the date opposite the Black Star and turn the *coming sign* (which is Aries on this circle) back to said date. We then refer to December 28th, and we find Mercury is in Taurus.

The Black Star on the Venus circle ends with Scorpio, so the coming sign is Sagittarius, on the Venus circle, and it must be turned back to that sign. On Mars the coming sign is Aries; on the Moon it is New Moon.

So watch the Black Star, and the coming sign in finding positions.

TABLE FOR SETTING THE DISKS OF THE CHART.

Mercury.				Venus.			Mars.			Moon.		
1825	Jan.	2	♉	Jan.	11	♉	Jan.	4	♐	Jan.	4	♈
1826	"	5	♌	"	1	♐	"	26	♎	"	24	"
1827	"	2	♎	"	11	♌	"	1	♈	"	15	"
1828	"	8	♐	"	1	♓	Feb.	19	♏	"	5	"
1829	"	6	♑	"	9	♏	Jan.	4	♉	"	26	"
1830	"	7	♒	"	1	♊	"	5	♏	"	18	"
1831	"	5	♈	"	10	♒	"	9	♊	"	6	"
1832	"	2	♊	"	1	♍	"	26	♐	"	23	"
1833	"	4	♍	"	10	♉	"	25	♋	"	10	"
1834	"	5	♏	"	1	♐	"	31	♑	"	24	"
1835	"	2	♐	"	10	♌	Feb.	14	♌	"	1	"
1836	"	1	♑	"	1	♓	"	10	♒	"	27	"
1837	"	6	♓	"	8	♏	Jan.	7	♌	"	7	"
1838	"	4	♉	"	1	♊	"	1	♒	"	25	"
1839	"	1	♋	"	9	♒	"	26	♍	"	6	"
1840	"	4	♎	"	1	♍	"	3	♓	"	24	"
1841	"	10	♐	"	9	♉	Feb.	15	♎	"	2	"
1842	"	9	♑	"	17	♑	Jan.	14	♈	"	21	"
1843	"	7	♒	"	9	♌	"	3	♎	"	1	"
1844	"	1	♓	"	18	♈	"	20	♉	"	19	"
1845	"	4	♊	"	8	♏	"	23	♏	"	10	"
1846	"	1	♌	"	17	♋	"	28	♊	"	27	"
1847	"	6	♏	"	8	♒	Feb.	10	♐	"	15	"
1848	"	5	♐	"	17	♎	"	12	♋	"	2	"
1849	"	2	♑	"	8	♉	Jan.	1	♐	"	20	"
1850	"	1	♒	"	17	♑	"	1	♋	"	7	"
1851	"	1	♈	"	8	♌	"	6	♑	"	25	"
1852	"	4	♋	"	16	♈	"	19	♌	"	14	"
1853	"	1	♍	"	7	♏	"	13	♒	"	3	"
1854	"	1	♏	"	17	♋	Feb.	11	♍	"	21	"
1855	"	11	♑	"	7	♒	Jan.	22	♓	"	9	"
1856	"	8	♒	"	17	♎	"	1	♍	"	27	"
1857	"	3	♓	"	8	♉	"	31	♈	"	15	"
1858	"	5	♊	"	16	♑	"	21	♎	"	4	"
1859	"	3	♌	"	7	♌	Feb.	7	♉	"	22	"
1860	"	1	♎	"	15	♈	"	10	♏	"	10	"
1861	"	6	♐	"	6	♏	"	13	♊	"	27	"
1862	"	5	♑	"	15	♋	Jan.	1	♏	"	16	"

Table for Setting the Disks of the Chart.—Continued.

Year	Mercury.		Venus.		Mars.		Moon.	
1863	Jan. 3	♒	Jan. 7	♒	Jan. 1	♊	Jan. 5	☉
1864	" 3	♈	" 16	♎	" 13	♐	" 24	"
1865	" 6	♋	" 7	♉	" 16	♋	" 12	"
1866	" 3	♍	" 15	♑	" 23	♑	" 29	"
1867	" 3	♏	" 6	♌	Feb. 6	♌	" 18	"
1868	" 1	♐	" 16	♈	" 1	♒	" 7	"
1869	" 11	♒	" 5	♏	Jan. 1	♌	" 23	"
1870	" 10	♈	" 15	♋	Feb. 8	♓	" 11	"
1871	" 2	♉	" 5	♒	Jan. 16	♍	" 28	"
1872	" 5	♌	" 15	♎	" 1	♓	" 18	"
1873	" 3	♎	" 6	♉	Feb. 6	♎	" 7	"
1874	" 9	♐	" 14	♑	Jan. 5	♈	" 27	"
1875	" 7	♑	" 6	♌	" 1	♎	" 16	"
1876	" 5	♒	" 15	♈	" 13	♉	" 3	"
1877	" 5	♈	" 4	♏	" 11	♏	" 22	"
1878	" 2	♊	" 14	♋	" 18	♊	" 10	"
1879	" 5	♍	" 5	♒	Feb. 2	♐	" 28	"
1880	" 4	♏	" 14	♎	" 4	♋	" 17	"
1881	" 3	♐	" 4	♉	" 9	♑	" 6	"
1882	" 1	♑	" 13	♑	" 23	♌	" 24	"
1883	" 7	♓	" 4	♌	Jan. 1	♑	" 13	"
1884	" 5	♉	" 14	♈	" 12	♌	" 2	"
1885	" 2	♋	" 3	♏	" 4	♒	" 20	"
1886	" 5	♎	" 13	♋	" 31	♍	" 8	"
1887	" 11	♐	" 4	♒	" 14	♓	" 26	"
1888	" 9	♑	" 13	♎	Feb. 22	♎	" 14	"
1889	" 7	♒	" 4	♉	Jan. 22	♈	" 2	"
1890	" 1	♓	" 13	♑	" 11	♎	" 21	"
1891	" 4	♊	" 4	♌	" 28	♉	" 9	"
1892	" 2	♌	" 13	♈	" 30	♏	" 27	"
1893	" 7	♏	" 2	♏	Feb. 5	♊	" 16	"
1894	" 5	♐	" 13	♋	" 19	♐	" 5	"
1895	" 3	♑	" 3	♒	" 19	♋	" 23	"
1896	" 2	♒	" 12	♎	Jan. 6	♐	" 10	"
1897	" 1	♈	" 3	♉	" 7	♋	" 27	"
1898	" 4	♋	" 11	♑	" 14	♑	" 16	"
1899	" 7	♎	" 3	♌	" 29	♌	" 4	"

Table for Placing the Four Outermost Planets Directly Upon the Zodiac Without Using the Chart.

Jupiter.	Saturn.	Uranus.	Neptune.
1825 Jan. 1 ♌	Jan. 1 ♊	Jan. 1 ♑	Jan. 1 ♑
1825 Nov. 1 ♍	....	....	....
1826 Oct. 22 ♎	....	....	....
1827 Nov. 21 ♏	Jan. 1 ♋	....	....
1828 Dec. 12 ♐	....	Jan. 1 ♒	....
1829 " 12 ♐	July 1 ♌	....	....
1830 Jan. 12 ♑	....	....	....
1831 " 1 ♒	May 15 ♍	....	....
1832 " 1 ♓	....	....	....
1832 Nov. 1 ♈	....	....	....
1833 Oct. 10 ♉	Oct. 1 ♎	....	....
1834 " 1 ♊	....	....	....
1835 Aug. 25 ♋	....	July 1 ♓	....
1836 Sept. 5 ♌	May 1 ♏	....	July 1 ♒
1837 " 5 ♍	....	....	....
1838 Oct. 1 ♎	Nov. 1 ♐	....	....
1839 " 5 ♏	....	....	....
1840 Nov. 10 ♐	....	....	....
1841 " 20 ♑	July 1 ♑	....	....
1842 Dec. 1 ♒	....	....	....
1843 Nov. 10 ♓	....	Jan. 1 ♈	....
1844 Oct. 12 ♈	Mar. 1 ♒	....	....
1845 Aug. 10 ♉	....	....	....
1846 July 15 ♊	Oct. 1 ♓	....	....
1847 June 20 ♋	....	....	....
1848 July 1 ♌	....	....	....
1849 " 1 ♍	June 1 ♈	....	....
1850 " 25 ♎	....	July 1 ♉	Jan. 1 ♓
1851 Aug. 10 ♏	Sept. 1 ♉	....	....
1852 " 15 ♐	....	....	....
1853 Oct. 1 ♑	Nov. 1 ♊	....	....
1854 Sept. 1 ♒	....	....	....
1855 Aug. 5 ♓	....	....	....
1856 " 3 ♈	Feb. 1 ♋	....	....
1857 July 5 ♉	....	....	....
1858 June 1 ♊	July 1 ♌	Jan. 1 ♊	....
1859 May 20 ♋	....	....	....
1860 " 10 ♌	Nov. 1 ♍	....	....
1861 " 20 ♍	....	....	....

Table for Placing the Four Outermost Planets Directly Upon the Zodiac Without Using the Chart.—Continued.

Jupiter.	Saturn.	Uranus.	Neptune.
1862 June 5 ♎	May 1 ♎	....	....
1863 July 1 ♏	....	....	July 1 ♈
1864 " 15 ♐	....	....	....
1865 Aug. 1 ♑	Aug. 1 ♏	Jan. 1 ♋	....
1866 July 25 ♒	....	....	....
1867 " 1 ♓	....	....	....
1868 June 10 ♈	Mar. 20 ♐	....	....
1869 May 7 ♉	....	....	....
1870 Apr. 1 ♊	Nov. 1 ♑	....	....
1871 Mar. 20 ♋	....	July 1 ♌	....
1872 " 1 ♌	....	....	....
1873 Apr. 1 ♍	June 20 ♒	....	....
1874 " 20 ♎	....	....	....
1875 May 20 ♏	....	....	....
1876 " 22 ♐	Jan. 15 ♓	....	....
1877 June 20 ♑	....	....	Jan. 1 ♉
1878 " 1 ♒	Oct. 1 ♈	Jan. 1 ♍	....
1879 May 8 ♓	....	....	....
1880 Apr. 10 ♈	....	....	....
1881 Mar. 22 ♉	Jan. 1 ♉	....	....
1882 Feb. 15 ♊	....	....	....
1883 Jan. 25 ♋	May 1 ♊	....	....
1884 " 15 ♌	....	Oct. 1 ♎	....
1885 Feb. 10 ♍	Sept. 1 ♋	....	....
1886 " 20 ♎	....	....	....
1887 Mar. 15 ♏	....	....	....
1888 Apr. 1 ♐	Jan. 1 ♌	....	....
1889 May 1 ♑	....	....	Oct. 1 ♊
1890 Apr. 1 ♒	Mar. 1 ♍	....	....
1891 Mar. 10 ♓	....	June 1 ♏	....
1892 Feb. 15 ♈	July 1 ♎	....	....
1893 Jan. 20 ♉	....	....	....
1894 " 10 ♊	....	....	....
1895 Jan. 1 ♋	Jan. 1 ♏	....	....
1896 Dec. 1 ♌	....	....	....
1897 Jan. 1 ♍	Sept. 1 ♐	....	....
1898 " 1 ♎	....	Sept. 1 ♐	....
1899 Feb. 1 ♏	....	....	....

TABLE OF PHYSICAL POWERS OF POSITION.

	♈	♉	♊	♋	♌	♍	♎	♏	♐	♑	♒	♓
Mercury,	21	24	24	24	21	18	15	12	9	12	15	18
Venus,	20	21	22	23	24	23	22	21	20	19	18	19
Mars,	20	18	16	14	12	10	12	14	16	18	20	22
Jupiter,	24	22	20	19	18	17	16	17	18	19	20	22
Saturn,	14	16	18	20	18	16	14	12	10	8	10	12
Uranus,	11	18	15	17	19	19	19	17	15	13	11	9
Neptune,	13	14	13	12	11	10	9	8	9	10	11	12
Earth,	4	5	6	7	6	5	4	3	2	1	2	3

RULE.—To find the physical power of a planet at any given time, add the number of its aspect to the Earth, to the power of position, multiply by three, and then add the co-ordinate power of the Earth's position, and the result will be the physical power of the planet's effect upon the Earth at the time. The same rule applies to the mental table. These rules are arranged to give the ruling stars after co-ordinating their mental and physical relations.

TABLE OF MENTAL POWERS OF POSITION.

	♈	♉	♊	♋	♌	♍	♎	♏	♐	♑	♒	♓
Mercury,	24	20	19	23	18	17	22	16	15	21	14	13
Venus,	22	18	17	21	16	15	20	14	13	19	12	11
Mars,	20	16	15	19	14	13	18	12	11	17	10	9
Jupiter,	18	14	13	17	12	11	16	10	9	15	8	7
Saturn,	16	12	11	15	10	9	14	8	7	13	6	5
Uranus,	14	10	9	13	8	7	12	6	5	11	4	3
Neptune,	12	8	7	11	6	5	10	4	3	9	2	1
Earth,	7	3	4	6	5	6	5	3	2	4	2	1

ASTRONOMICAL FIGURES.

To bring the dimensions and relations of the planets of our solar system within the comprehension of mortals, it is necessary to construct a system in the mind made up from physical bodies with which we are familiar. Astronomy gives an illustration something like this:

Imagine yourself stationed in the center of a large field or prairie beside a ball 4 feet 8 inches in diameter, to represent the Sun. Now, imagine a ball about the size of an ordinary pea or current, placed on the circumference of a circle 194 feet from the large ball representing the Sun. This will illustrate the distance from, and comparative size of the planet Mercury to the Sun. On a circle 362 feet from the Sun, place an ordinary cherry to represent the beautiful magnet Venus. A ball about the same size should be placed 500 feet from the center to represent the Earth.

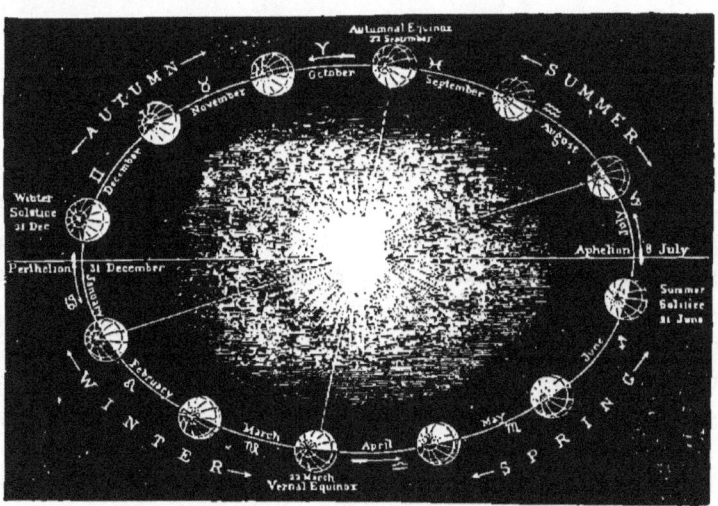

The Orbit of the Earth as seen by an observer at the Sun.

Next in order is Mars, and in comparison would be about the size of a large currant, and should be on a circle 762 feet away from the Sun. A belt of planetoids come next which would be represented best by grains of sand and gravel about equally divided around a circle one-quarter mile distant from the center. Jupiter, by a globe about the size of a large cocoanut, 5½ inches in diameter, on the circumference of a circle distant from the Sun about one-half mile. A ball 4½ inches in diameter, inside of a small hoop 7 inches in diameter, would illustrate Saturn and his rings, and should be about one mile away. An ordinary orange will fill the place of Uranus at a distance of nearly two miles from the Sun. Neptune is somwhat larger than Uranus and must be placed nearly three miles away in order to illustrate the immense distance of that magnet from the central Orb.

Now for the Moons: Take a ball about as large as the head of an ordinary pin and place it on a circle 16 inches from the Earth to represent our Moon on its orbit. Jupiter's four large moons, being each the size of Mercury, would be represented by small currants, on circles around Jupiter and distant from it—the first, 18⅔ inches; the second, 29¼ inches; the third, 46¾ inches; and the fourth, 80 inches (6⅔ feet). Saturn's eight moons would be represented by small currants, the one farthest from Saturn being about the size of Mercury, the others growing smaller as they approach it and on circles distant from it—the first, 8 inches; the second, 10 inches; the third, 12½ inches; the fourth, 16 inches; the fifth, 22 3-5 inches; the sixth, 52 inches; the seventh, 62⅔ inches; and the eighth, 12 feet 7 inches. Four of the moons of Uranus would have to be represented about the same as those of Saturn and on circles distant from it—the first, 8 feet and 8 inches; the second, 52 inches; the third, 25 inches; the fourth,

19 inches. Neptune's one known moon would be represented on a circle about 15 inches from it. These figures give the relative sizes and distances of the stars composing our solar system.

What does this imaginary system represent? First, this ball 4 feet 8 inches in diameter represents a ball that is really 852,584 miles in diameter. The first small pea or currant, Mercury, is 2,962 miles in diameter and 35,329,638 miles from the Sun. The diameter of Venus is 7,510 miles. Venus is distant from the Sun 66,131,478 miles, and the Earth about the same in size is distant 91,430,220 miles. Mars has a diameter of 4,920 miles and is distant from the Sun 139,312,226 miles. The great Jupiter, with a diameter of about 88,390 miles, is distant from the Sun 475,693,149 miles. Saturn has a diameter of 77,904 miles, with its rings extending on all sides about 50,000 miles farther, making the diameter about 170,000 miles. It is distant from the Sun 872,134,583 miles. Uranus' diameter is 33,024 miles, and is distant from the Sun 1,753,-851,052 miles. Neptune, with a diameter of 36,620 miles and a distance from the Sun of 2,746,271,232 miles; giving the solar system a diameter of 5,492,542,464 miles. The planets make the circuit of their respective orbits: Mercury in 88 days; Venus in 224 days; Earth in one year, 365 days; Mars in 687 days; Jupiter in 11 years, 10 months, and 17 days; Saturn in about 29½ years; Uranus in about 84 years; and Neptune in 164 years. The solar system thus appears to be very large, but is only relatively so. As compared with the Earth and earthly things, it is large; but compared with the small cluster of 16,000,000 suns and all their attendant planets to which we belong, it is very small indeed.

Relative Sizes of the Planets.

With such wonderful calculations concerning the magnitudes and relations of the planets in our solar system, well may we inquire how are we, as human beings, related to these heavenly magnets. Professor Proctor, the celebrated astronomer, has stated that the planet Neptune, 2,750,000,000 miles from the Sun, vibrates and trembles like a reed in the wind whenever great magnetic and electrical storms are raging upon the Sun. This being true, there must be a very intimate relation existing between our Earth and that wonderful Orb, and the electrical and magnetic currents are the basis of calculations for much of the phenomena transpiring all about us.

"Where are the souls to whom the spectacle of a starry night is not an eloquent discourse? Where are those who have not been sometimes arrested in the presence of the bright worlds which hover over our heads, and who have not sought for the key of the great enigma of creation? The solitary hours of night are in truth the most beautiful of all our hours. The Orb of day hides from our view the grandeur of the firmament; it is during the night that we are able to communicate with the great starry spheres, encircling our earthly home."

Without beginning and without end is this vast expanse of apparent space which surrounds us, yet rapid are the changes that are constantly taking place.

Worlds are born, developed, and brought to their highest estate for the expression of soul life, when they begin to decline, and finally become dead and cold material magnets, to be re-constructed, re-vivified, in coming cycles to take their place again in a "new heaven, (as) new earths."

The great weather prophets, Balot, Hornburg, Zadkiel, Mansill, Hicks, and many others, base their calculations upon this occult relation, magnetic and electrical, which binds the planets of our solar system together, as with cables of steel, and their prognostications concerning the weather, although not absolute, are very wonderful. The weather, however, cannot be located accurately by astronomical calculations, as it is principally atmospherical, although the magnetic and electrical currents have a bearing, in producing atmospheric disturbances. But to locate a storm is beyond the calculations of men. The human organism has wonderful electrical and magnetic forces which are little understood by the majority of people; but many scientific minds are investigating the wonderful magnetic relation existing between human beings, who are human magnets, and planetary beings, which are planetary magnets; and "The Law and the Prophets" is designed to give the truth concerning these relations and influences in the simplest and shortest method possible.

CONCLUSION.

As I conclude to finish this work and write "the end" at the bottom of this page, a million pages come up before me for recognition, and statement. My soul yearns for more time and more space with which to explain the meaning of law, the meaning of life, the meaning of wisdom, the meaning of power, the meaning of eternal happiness, contentment and satisfaction, which is found in the inner sanctum, sanctorum, that abideth forever within the soul. I hope that every one who reads this work will become a teacher, and assist in elevating the human race to a higher standard. My work is done. Take it, O! mortals, and use it,—"For the harvest is abundant and the laborers are few."

F. E. ORMSBY.

CHICAGO, 1893.

THE END.

www.ingramcontent.com/pod-product-compliance
Lightning Source LLC
Chambersburg PA
CBHW021732220426
43662CB00008B/814